Transitioning Into A Software Development Manager

Scan for all books from the author

MOHAMMAD MASUD

Copyright © 2022 by Mohammad Masud.

Published On Amazon Kindle Direct Publishing (KDP).

Edited for correction and for clarity on March 18th, 2023
Reprinted with correction on February 5th, 2023
Published on December 31st, 2022
ISBN: 979-8-835-73218-0 (Paperback)
ISBN: 979-8-370-88670-6 (Hardcover)

Thank you -

Asif Yusuf Russo (DCL)
Mohammed J. Kabir (Evoknow Inc.)
Mohammed Bakhtiar (Core Team, IBBL)
Golam Kibria (Grameenphone)
Richard Scannell (State Street Corp)
Ashwin Kasturi (State Street Corp)
Larry Hodgman (State Street Corp)
And many more…

I am indebted to all my managers throughout my career from whom I learned many of these technology and management skills covered in this book, directly or indirectly!

Special thanks to my daughter Fatima Faiza; every time she touches the manuscript, my book flows smoother.

P.S. She edited this dedication too!

Table of Contents

PREFACE — 12

INTRODUCTION — 18

WHAT'S UNIQUE ABOUT MANAGING SOFTWARE DEVELOPERS? — 19
WHEN IS THE TIME TO TRANSITION? — 20
ROADMAP OF THE JOURNEY — 21
DEVELOPER — 21
DEVELOPMENT TEAM LEAD — 22
DEVELOPMENT MANAGER — 24
NON-SOFTWARE DEVELOPMENT ROLES — 26

CHAPTER 1: SOFTWARE DEVELOPMENT MANAGER — 28

SPECTRUM OF MANAGER'S ROLE — 29
HIRING — 29
HIRING MANAGEMENT: — 30
HIRING STEPS: — 30
BUDGETING AND FORECASTING — 31
CREATING TEAM — 32
BUILDING TEAM — 33
Stages in Building a Team — 35
MANAGING THE SDLC — 36
PERFORMANCE MANAGEMENT — 36
TEAM PERFORMANCE — 38
INDIVIDUAL PERFORMANCE — 40
Reward and Recognition — 40

FIRING	42
FIRING MANAGEMENT	42

CHAPTER 2: MANAGER AS A LEADER — 45

TECHNOLOGY LEADERSHIP	46
STRATEGIC LEADERSHIP	47

CHAPTER 3: PEOPLE SKILLS OF A MANAGER — 50

CRITICAL THINKING	51
EFFECTIVE DECISION MAKING	52
MOTIVATING	59
EFFECTIVE COMMUNICATION	60
EFFECTIVE NEGOTIATION	61
MANAGING CONFLICTS	63
EFFECTIVE DELEGATION	64
EFFECTIVE LISTENING	66
EMOTIONAL INTELLIGENCE AND SECOND-ORDER THINKING	67
CONSTRUCTIVE FEEDBACK ESSENTIALS	68
FUEL INNOVATION AND CREATIVITY	69
INFLUENCE COURAGEOUSLY	70
FACILITATION AND EFFECTIVE MEETINGS	72
NETWORKING AND BUILDING RELATIONSHIPS	73
MENTORING	76
COACHING	77
MANAGING WORKING REMOTE	78
PROJECT AND ORGANIZATION	81

CHAPTER 4: SOFTWARE PROJECT MANAGEMENT — 83

PROJECT ORIENTED MANAGEMENT	88
PROJECT INITIATION	88
PROJECT PLANNING	89
PROJECT EXECUTION	91
PROJECT MONITORING & CONTROLLING	91
PROJECT CLOSURE	93
PRODUCT ORIENTED MANAGEMENT	**94**

CHAPTER 5: SOFTWARE DEVELOPMENT METHODOLOGIES — 96

WATERFALL DEVELOPMENT METHODOLOGY	98
ITERATIVE DEVELOPMENT PROCESS	101
AGILE	103
AGILE SOFTWARE DEVELOPMENT	103
Myth and Truth about Agile	104
How to reap the best out of Agile	106
Scrum	111
Extreme Programming (XP)	112
Pair Programming	112
Test-Driven Development	113
SCALING AGILE	113
SCALED AGILE FRAMEWORK (SAFE)	113
Spotify Model	115
HYBRID SDLC	**116**
DESIGN THINKING	**117**
MYTHS AND TRUTHS OF COLLOCATION	**120**

CHAPTER 6: SOFTWARE DESIGN REVIEW — 123

CREATE A VERY HIGH-LEVEL DESIGN (HLD)	125
DETAIL ARCHITECTURE & DESIGN	126

DESIGN REVIEW	126
CHAPTER 7: DEEP DIVE INTO AGILE SCRUM	**129**
HOW (AND WHY) TO BUILD A SCRUM TEAM	**131**
PEOPLE	131
TEAM BUILDING	133
SCRUM TEAM ROLES	**133**
PRODUCT OWNER	133
SCRUM MASTER (SM)	134
DEVELOPER	134
SCRUM ARTIFACTS	**135**
USER STORY	135
USER STORY TASK	136
PRODUCT BACKLOG (PB)	137
SPRINT BACKLOG	138
DEFINITION OF READY (DOR)	138
DEFINITION OF DONE (DOD)	139
BURNDOWN CHART	139
SPRINT VELOCITY	140
SCRUM CADENCE	**140**
SPRINT	141
PRODUCT BACKLOG GROOMING	141
SPRINT PLANNING	142
DAILY SCRUM	143
SCRUM DEMO OR SCRUM REVIEW	144
SCRUM RETROSPECTIVE	145
SCRUM PRE-REQUISITES	145
MYTH OF SOFTWARE ARCHITECTURE IN SCRUM	**146**
CHAPTER 8: SOFTWARE REQUIREMENT MANAGEMENT	**148**

REQUIREMENT MANAGEMENT	**149**
REQUIREMENT ANALYSIS	**149**
OBJECT-ORIENTED ANALYSIS	149
USE CASE	150
USER STORY	150
TRIANGULATION IN SOFTWARE REQUIREMENTS	**150**
SOFTWARE COST ESTIMATION	**152**
THE CONE OF UNCERTAINTY	154
STANDARD ESTIMATION MODELS AND METHODS	156
Line of Code (LOC/SLOC)	157
COCOMO	157
Function Point Analysis	158
Use Case Points Method (UUCPM)	159
User Story Points (USP)	160
Delphi Method	161
Heuristic Method	162
CHOOSE THE RIGHT ESTIMATION MODEL	163
SOFTWARE ESTIMATION BEST PRACTICES	164
CHAPTER 9: SOFTWARE QUALITY MANAGEMENT	**168**
SQA PROCESS	**169**
CREATE TEST STRATEGY	170
CREATE TEST PLAN	170
CREATE TEST CASE AND TEST SCENARIO	170
CREATE TEST ENVIRONMENT	170
TEST DATA MANAGEMENT	170
EXECUTE TEST	171
COMMUNICATE TEST RESULT	171
HOW MUCH TESTING IS ENOUGH FOR SOFTWARE?	172
ALTERNATIVE STRATEGIES OF SOFTWARE TESTING	**174**

RISK-WEIGHTED TESTING	174
CHANGE ORIENTED TESTING	175
USAGE-DRIVEN TESTING	176
DEBUGGING IS MORE OF AN ART THAN SCIENCE	**177**
SOFTWARE CONFIDENCE INDEX (SCI)	**180**

CHAPTER 10: TECH SKILLS OF A MANAGER — 188

SOFTWARE ARCHITECTURE & DESIGN	**189**
N-TIER ARCHITECTURE AND LAYERED ARCHITECTURE	**190**
SERVICE-ORIENTED ARCHITECTURE (SOA)	**190**
MICROSERVICES ARCHITECTURE	**191**
SOLID PRINCIPLE	**192**
OBJECT-ORIENTED DESIGN	**194**
INHERITANCE	194
ENCAPSULATION	194
POLYMORPHISM	194
DESIGN PATTERN	195
OBJECT-ORIENTED DESIGN PATTERNS	195
UNIFIED MODELING LANGUAGE	195
SYSTEM DESIGN	**196**
APPLICATION SCALABILITY	197
CLEAN CODING SKILLS	**199**
REFACTORING	**200**

CHAPTER 11: DEVOPS AND INFRASTRUCTURE — 203

CONFIGURATION MANAGEMENT	204
CONTINUOUS INTEGRATION	204
CLOUD COMPUTING INFRASTRUCTURE	205
TYPES OF CLOUDS	205
Private Cloud	206

Public Cloud	206
Hybrid Cloud	206
TOPOLOGY	206
Software as a Service (SaaS)	207
Platform as a Service (PaaS)	207
Infrastructure as a Service	207
AWS - pioneer and market leader in public Cloud computing	207
DEV OPS	209

CHAPTER 12: SOFTWARE SECURITY — 211

THE GOAL OF SOFTWARE SECURITY	212
PHASES OF SECURE SOFTWARE DEVELOPMENT	213
PLANNING	213
EXECUTION	216
MONITORING	219
CONTROLLING	221

CHAPTER 13: THE ART OF SOFTWARE DEVELOPMENT — 223

PROJECT INITIATION	224
USER EXPERIENCE	226
REQUIREMENT GATHERING	227
ARCHITECTURE AND DESIGN	228
DEVELOPMENT AND TESTING	228
SOFTWARE QUALITY ASSURANCE	229
BUILD AND DEPLOYMENT	230
RELEASE MANAGEMENT	230
OPERATIONAL EXCELLENCE	230
DEBUGGING	231

CHAPTER 14: THE ART OF SOFTWARE DEVELOPMENT MANAGEMENT — 232

TECHNOLOGY LEADERSHIP — 233
TEAM BUILDING — 233
TRUST — 236
RESPECT — 236
LEAD BY EXAMPLE — 237
DECISION MAKING THROUGH CONSULTATION — 237
TECHNICAL PROWESS — 240
COMMUNICATION — 240
RELATIONSHIP — 241
METRICS BASED MANAGEMENT — 242
MANAGING TEAM THROUGH GOALS — 243
BEWARE OF DEVELOPER'S HOUR VS. MANAGER'S HOUR — 243
MULTITASKING: MYTH AND TRUTH — 244
COLLECTIVE (TEAM) KNOWLEDGE — 245
OTHER COMMONLY OCCURRING BEST PRACTICES — 245

CHAPTER 15: ETHICAL SOFTWARE DEVELOPMENT — 249

MYTH OF JOB SECURITY — 251
REQUIREMENT — 252
ARCHITECTURE AND DESIGN — 253
CODING — 255
DOCUMENTATION — 255

REFERENCES — 256

INDEX — 258

Preface

This book is designed for software professionals, like you, who have already established themselves as successful in the technical landscape. If you are now facing the opportunity (or challenge) of managing a team of other technical professionals, you may find that managing people who design, code, and deploy software is completely different from managing your own designs, architectures, and code. While technology is more objective and predictable in nature, managing people requires an understanding of their psychology and unique personalities.

Assuming that you are reading this book because you are facing the complexity of a large-scale solution technology stack that requires a well-managed team to deliver the solution, it is important to note that managerial soft skills are expected of you as you move into a management role. This book has been created with that purpose in mind. By the time you finish reading it, you will have gained the necessary skills to successfully manage such a team.

There are several paths you can take to learn management, such as earning a management degree, paying for online courses, or reading management books, articles, and tutorials to learn from the experiences of others in the field. If you are able to take one of these paths, then you may not need this book, and I wish you the best of luck in your journey. Personally, I took this route for years before taking on my first management role. However, the transition to a management position is often a significant leap in one's career, leaving many people unsure of where to begin.

You may not be uncertain about the route to take, but you may lack the time to spend years acquiring management skills while also honing your technical skills. On the other hand, you may be willing to dedicate years to learning, but your new management position may start very soon. Regardless of your circumstances, preparing oneself for a management role can be challenging, and there may be limited options available. Moreover, even if you learn management skills from "standard" management books, you may face difficulties in applying those skills to managing software engineers, who are a unique breed of professionals. Their work requires specific technical skills, and managing them demands a distinct set of people skills that traditional management books may not cover.

If you also believe that software development is a unique profession and managing developers has unique aspects to it, then this book is written for you. However, regardless of why you are reading this book, you are likely one of the smartest technical engineers in your organization. Unfortunately, it is a common but counterproductive practice for organizations to recognize their smartest developers by promoting them to a management position that requires more people skills than coding skills. For many of these individuals, the transition can be a nightmare.

It is often assumed that those who successfully manage technologies and lead developers are also capable of managing software developers. However, this assumption disregards the fundamental difference between managing technologies and managing people. The skills required for managing people are fundamentally different from those needed for managing technologies, and they cannot be transferred in every aspect. People management demands certain technical skills that are essential for effective management.

The absence of necessary people skills and an overabundance of technical skills will not only affect the development team but also hinder the new manager's career aspirations. To understand why your success as a developer may not be enough to transition seamlessly into management, I recommend reading the book "*What Got You Here Won't Get You There*" by Marshall Goldsmith.

It is essential to have the necessary people management skills to realize the full potential of a software development team. The objective of this book is to provide training on both people management skills and technical management skills required to be effective in a managerial role. By equipping oneself with the necessary skills, one can effectively manage software engineers and lead them towards success.

As with any other discipline, each technical and management skill can be a topic of its own, with its own dedicated chapter or even a full book. However, to achieve the objective of this book, I will provide you with the most common practical ideas for each topic, and provide a simplified method for applying them. Consider these ideas as primers that will help you appreciate management skills, and allow you to decide which areas of skills require a deeper dive, or if you're ready to start managing your team from "tomorrow".

This book will give you a solid foundation to build on, and encourage you to explore specific management skills through other articles and books. As you progress through each chapter, I'll also point you towards reference materials, tutorials, and books for further reading.

Part-I: *Management aspects of Software Development* and Part-II: *People aspects of Management* of the book, covers all the necessary management skills that are essential for a manager. It starts with setting the stage of what it means to be a technical manager and subsequently the necessary people skills are covered. Those skills aren't presented merely like "regular" management skills but spotlighted appropriately to meet the needs of a Software Development Manager.

The Part-III: *Process aspects of Management* and Part-IV: *Technology aspects of Management* of the book covers the Process and Technical aspects of the Software Developer management, to be more accurate, it covers- what it takes to develop a software. However, I have only chosen the topics that you absolutely need to know as a technical manager. You may ask, why would you read technicalities of software development from a management book? Two reasons: as software development is a highly technical field, you would need to show your technical and process knowledge superiority if you want them to feel that you're of the same breed like them hence gain their "technical" acceptance in the team. Absence of that, you would be more of an HR Manager of software engineers rather than an effective Software Development Manager. But the more important part is, even those technical skills are described from the perspective of a manager instead of an individual contributor and spot-lighted appropriately. The Part-III: *Process aspects of Management* is written to cover all the processes to manage a software development team or project. So, even though you were exposed to those processes at your work, I suggest you pay attention to them. For Part-IV: *Technology aspects of Management*, I highly recommend at least skimming through the chapters even if you may know most of it. I promise you'll find something new. However, if you are not from a serious software development background or if you feel you don't have full grip in some areas and need further deep dive, you are welcome to start from those chapters. I have given enough resources and reading references for further learning. However, if you came from a software development background and transitioned into management, I would argue that you would be just fine with the depth of the technical topics covered in this book.

In addition to the comprehensive coverage of management skills for software development managers, this book also provides many nuggets of forewarnings about common pitfalls or misunderstandings of frequently used management practices. These are tagged with the icon (⚠) for easy reference throughout the book. The aim is to create awareness that there are no management skills that do not come with pitfalls. As a manager, inevitably you will self-identify those pitfalls over a period of time; however, as a new manager, knowing about these early in your career will help you avoid costly trial-and-error cycles.

Essentially, this book will work as a navigation system to take you to the journey of a software development manager and safely reach you to the destination. Once you complete this book, you should feel confident to achieve the most important outcome of management: bring predictability, repeatability and sustainability in your software development organization. Shape your own management style from there.

It's important to clarify who shouldn't read this book. It's not a comprehensive book about learning all general management skills in academic detail, as it frequently delves into software development when discussing general management practices. Similarly, it's not the book for someone who wants to start their professional career as a software developer. For that, there is another book available on Amazon.com (https://www.amazon.com/dp/B08BDSDYFL) called *"Transitioning into Professional Software Development"*:

To help you jump start, I have added frequently used several management templates available on the GitHub repository - The Manager's Aid templates:

https://github.com/TransitioningSoftwareDevelopment/SoftwareDevelopmentManager

How to contact

You are most welcome to provide feedback and suggestions to improve this book. Please visit the book's Facebook page: https://www.facebook.com/TransitioningIntoProSoftwareDevelopment/.

You can email the author for any question, comment or suggestions at mmasud.author.tsd@gmail.com.

Best of luck!

PART I

Management *aspects of* Software Development

Introduction

What's unique about managing software developers?

According to Merriam-Webster, management is defined as 'the act or art of managing: the conducting or supervising of something (such as a business).' While management has been used for thousands of years, it became an indispensable academic discipline during the industrial era, and it remains a vital part of everyday business, including software development.

However, managing software development is distinct from managing other areas such as manufacturing, construction, finance, or marketing. One may wonder if the same management knowledge and skills would suffice for a Software Development Manager to jump-start their career. After all, scientific management was formulated in the late nineteenth century, and management has been taught in colleges and universities for decades, with Harvard Business School being the first to offer a Master of Business Administration in 1921 to teach modern management theories.

Nevertheless, software development management has subtle yet distinct features that make it unique compared to general management. Therefore, it deserves special attention to learn the specific aspects of software development management:

- Software development is a field of creativity, like painting, sculpting, and performing arts, where solving the same problem using the same technology is rare.
- People management is an integral part of managing, but software developers and engineers, by nature, are creative and independent. They don't like to be confined to a rigid structure, much like performing artists. Hence, taking orders from managers is not their preference.
- Software developers take pride in their work and often boast about their technical prowess. As a result, earning their respect as a manager is challenging. If they cannot respect you as their leader, it will be an uphill battle to influence and manage them effectively. This is the reality, much like gravity, and ignoring it will only make your management task more difficult, if not impossible. Essentially, they want you to be as good as them to manage them effectively.

- The market for recruiting talented software engineers is very competitive, and retaining them for a long time is equally challenging. Due to the intense demand for talented software engineers, your margin for error is small. Therefore, if you're not skilled enough to handle software engineers, your chance of success diminishes. Moreover, if you work in a large company, you would be in a constant battle to retain talent in your team. To attract smart engineers to your team, you must build your brand as a charismatic Software Development Manager.

When is the time to transition?

You can set the time on your own terms when you want to start the journey of a Software Development Manager. However, my goal is to empower you with the knowledge and tools so that you can self-assess the right time to step into that role. You may have heard that success is not only about what you do but also about the timing and the environment. Therefore, I will primarily explain the "time" factor and briefly touch upon the "place" factor to help you make an informed decision. As you have already learned what's unique about managing software developers, you should ask yourself to self-assess whether the following statements describe your personality:

- You find it exciting, rather than intimidating, to talk to technical people to solve their problems.
- You can resist the temptation to jump into writing code for them and are comfortable reading others' code when they are stuck or when they can't figure out the bug in the code.
- You appreciate the value of an organic structure within an organization and recognize how it can leverage the power of people and technology to create a multiplier effect in building great software.

If these statements reflect your professional career aspiration, then you may be ready to jump right into the journey of a software development manager.

Introduction

Roadmap of the journey

The journey towards becoming a Software Development Manager can start from any position in your career, whether as a Developer, Development Lead, or Team Lead. Your focus and scope of learning would vary depending on your current role. I'll highlight these areas so you can use them as a navigation map. I highly recommend going through each of these roles before jumping into the manager role, but if the team is small and the scope is manageable, you may overlap some roles. However, for some people, people skills come naturally, and they may find it easier to jump into the manager role from the Developer role by skipping intermediate roles.

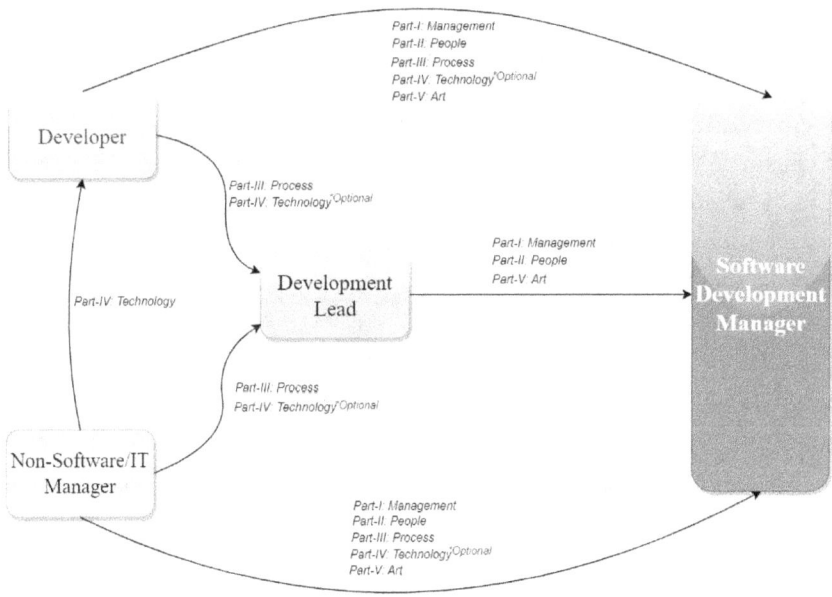

Figure-1: Depiction of the journey towards the Software Development Manager role

Developer

If you're a developer and an individual contributor, you're starting from the farthest end of the software development profession. At this stage, you're focused on gaining technical skills, interacting with other team members, and collaborating with others. You're assigned tasks as part of the project and you sprint to accomplish them. Once you complete your tasks, your team lead will give you further work assignments. You're not exposed to team planning, interpersonal issues, or team dynamics. As you embark on the journey to become a Software Development Manager, you'll start to expand your horizon from this stage. Here are the steps you should take from here:

- Master all the technical skills required for a Software Development Manager. These skills are a subset of technical skills that a developer should already be using in their day-to-day work. However, if you find any gaps in your technical skills, learn and apply them, as they're essential for being an effective manager.
- Besides bridging the gaps, you should pick up a new perspective from those technical skills. As a manager, most of the time, you'll be in a supervising role instead of doing the technical work yourself.
- Once you're fully equipped with the necessary technical skills, go back to the chapters on management skills. You're expected to have been on the receiving side of those skills most of the time, and now you'll see how to use them. Once you learn those skills, you're ready to apply them. It's recommended to go through another hop, i.e., Development Lead, before taking up the managerial role. But, if you're forced to fill that role without any choice, feel confident that you have the fundamentals to give it a shot.

Reminder ⚠: The basic skills required to start the journey are covered in this book. However, each of the skills can be an entire chapter or even a book. So, to save the book from becoming too voluminous or doing a disservice to the scholars of each area, I have given necessary references. Once you master those fundamentals and grow into your managerial role, you should go through those references (books/tutorials) given there and deep dive into them one at a time.

Development Team Lead

This is the stepping stone for a developer towards the Software Development Manager role. At this stage, you start to acquire many soft skills that are necessary to be a good leader. These skills can often be used as-is when you get into a management role. You could argue that at this stage of your career, you're playing the role of a pre-manager. Let's utilize this stage effectively to create a solid foundation for your successful management career

Here's a contrasting picture where a Dev Team Lead differs from a Dev manager from the perspective of a Dev Team Lead:

- As a Dev Team Lead, you may be given an already established team to lead. Even if you have the opportunity to build your own team, you typically are not responsible for hiring team members from within the organization or externally. If you find yourself in a position where you are responsible for hiring, you may be functioning as a manager without holding the official title.
- You contribute in creating project estimation working with the product and/or project manager. For initial high-level estimation, you may ask to provide a ballpark number. Subsequently you would be working with your team for proper estimation.
- You may be responsible for designing the technical solution architecture for your team. You may do it by yourself or work with a Solution Architect to create one based on your organization's structure.
- Depending on your SDLC and unless your team is self-organized due to the fact of being "true" Scrum or otherwise, you will be assigning development tasks to your team members.
- You do Design Review, Code Review, and take the most critical or complex implementations and deliver those side by side with your team members.
- You coordinate the user acceptance testing, triage the defects identified by users or QA engineers and appropriately assign/coordinate the fix.
- You participate in the build, deployment and promotion of software to the production environment. If you have DevOps as part of your team, you are often in the position of leading them otherwise you get it done through them.

Now comes to the soft skills that are in play as Dev Team Lead:

- You use effective delegation techniques to delegate many of your development related work to the team members.
- You are the first line of defense for conflict resolution. Mostly it would be technical related but sometimes the behavioral conflicts may be camouflaged as technical conflict so you need to be aware of that. If it becomes a complex and truly behavioral conflict, you would be passing that to the Project Manager or Development Manager.
- Apart from that, you would find yourself (explicitly or implicitly) using the following soft skills on-and-off depending on the scale of the team and breadth of your role in the team: Effective Communication, Effective Listening, Effective Decision Making, Relationships and Networking, Negotiation (to a lesser extent), and Facilitation, etc. These skills are covered in the subsequent chapter in detail so do not worry if you are not familiar with those management jargons.

Once you acquire a few more managerial skills, you'll pretty much ready to start the role of a Software Development Manager. So, what are the steps you should take from here? Here are a few recommendations:

- Continue through the Part-I: *Management aspects of Software Development*, Part-II: *People aspects of Management*, and Part-III: *Process aspects of Management* chapters to fill the gaps that you have in people and process skills.
- You may be tempted to skip the Part-IV: *Technology aspects of Management*, and I wouldn't blame you if you do, however, I strongly recommend you to skim through the topics, especially the Architecture and Design aspects of the technical skills.
- Finally, go through the chapters in the Part-V: *Art aspects of Management* in detail. These are best practices to help you transition into the role more smoothly.

Development Manager

If you're currently working as a Software Developer Manager, it means that you have successfully transitioned into this role. However, if you're still reading this book, I'm assuming that you may have been forced into this role, or you're not yet comfortable with it, or you want to improve your management skills further. If you've been promoted to this role as a reward for your success as a Developer or Development Lead, you are essentially still in a technical role and need to follow the transition route from that role. Therefore, it's recommended that you go back to the previous sections of Developer or Development Lead and plan your journey. However, if you're already in this role and you feel that you lack the necessary skills or want to improve your management skills further to grow in your career, here's a navigation map that can help you be successful in this role:

- Congratulations on accepting that you need to learn new techniques and skills to be successful. This is a crucial step because often, we fail to learn new skills as we falsely believe that we already possess them or do not need them. By acknowledging that there is a need to learn new skills, you have overcome the biggest obstacle. Well done!
- Next, go over the chapters in *Part-I: Management aspects of Software Development* & *Part-II: People aspects of Management* and create a checklist on what are the managerial skills that you are missing or not fully confident with. You can also prioritize the skills that you want to acquire.
- For technical skills, you are expected to have acquired all the necessary skills through your past career as a developer. However, it's possible that you may not have been exposed to some of the technical skills in your previous role. As a manager, your role has now changed or expanded, so you need to look at those same skills through a different lens. You need to master some of them further, while others you will be supervising instead of doing on your own. To bridge any gaps in your technical knowledge and gain a manager's perspective on those technologies, read through Part IV: Technology Aspects of Management.
- Once you have your list of skills (or a prioritized list), read about each skill, understand its importance, and learn how to apply it in your job. Remember that simply reading about a skill is not enough, you need to practice it in your day-to-day job to master it.
- To save time, use the templates available on the *Manager's Aid* the GitHub repository. You can tailor them to meet your organization's

needs, but not using them may slow down your progress in effectively using those skills.
- Assess your progress against the skills you planned to improve. Course-correct if needed and reassess priorities.
- Once you have mastered the foundational managerial skills, you can move on to the next level of expertise. You can find resources such as books and articles in the references section to advance your skills as a manager.
- Finally, go through the chapters in *Part V: Art Aspects of Management* in detail. These chapters contain best practices that can help you expedite your transition into the role.

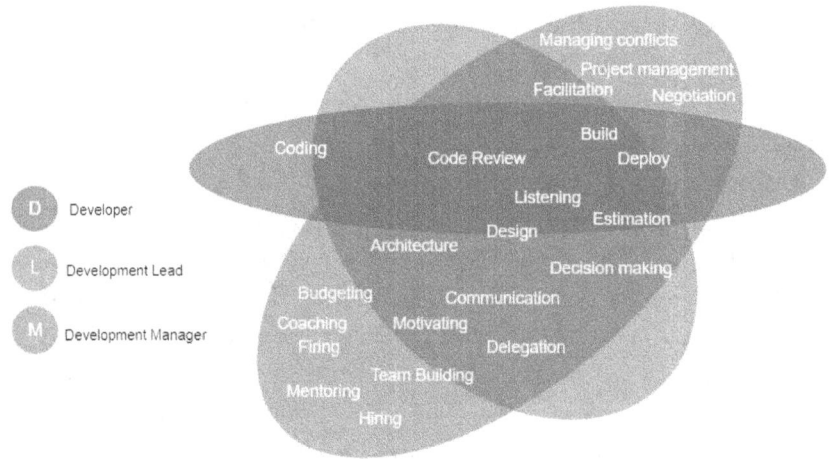

Figure-2: Venn diagram showing the skills of Software Developer, Development Lead and a Development Manager

Non-Software Development roles

If you're coming from a non-software development field, such as IT Manager, and want to switch to software development as a manager, you'll need to start from the beginning of the book and go all the way to the end. This book is organized in a way that covers the skills required for a Software Development Manager in a relevant and sequential manner.

As a non-software development professional, it's essential to retain and build upon your existing skills while also learning to see them through a manager's lens. This will help you understand how to apply these skills in a software development context. You'll also need to acquire new skills to fill any gaps in your knowledge.

By following the guidance in this book, you'll be well-prepared to thrive in the dynamic world of managing software development at scale. Remember to assess your progress regularly and make any necessary course corrections to ensure that you're continuously improving your skills as a manager.

Congratulations, you've equipped yourself with the necessary roadmap to become a successful software development manager. You're now ready to step into the zone and make a significant impact in this dynamic and rewarding role. Welcome aboard, and get ready to unleash your full potential!

Chapter 1: Software Development Manager

Spectrum of Manager's role

While there may be an academic definition of what a manager does, the specific responsibilities of a manager can vary depending on the stage of their career and the structure of the organization. As a Software Development Manager, you may find yourself responsible for anything from hiring to firing, or anywhere in between on the management spectrum.

Regardless of where you fall on the spectrum, it is important to have a clear understanding of the full range of management responsibilities so that you can plan for career progression and effectively fulfill your role as a manager. In this article, we will cover the various areas that fall within the management spectrum and provide you with insights and guidance to help you succeed in your role as a Software Development Manager.

Hiring

While hiring may be the first item on the managerial spectrum, as a Software Development Manager, you may not start with this responsibility in the early stages of your career. Hiring requires a combination of skills such as budgeting and forecasting, effective decision making, negotiation, effective communication, team building, effective delegation, networking, and more. It can be a challenging responsibility that takes time and experience to master.

In most cases, your senior manager will take the lead in the hiring process, gradually involving you in the process over time. You may start as a panelist in the interview process, but owning the end-to-end process of hiring may come later as you gain experience and confidence in your managerial abilities. It is important to recognize that this responsibility requires a high level of skill and experience, and it is okay to take a gradual approach to developing this area of expertise.

Whether you have recently taken on the responsibility of a hiring manager, or have been dropped into an end-to-end management role from day one due to the size of the company or other practical reasons, going through the management spectrum can provide valuable insights and strategies for success. Even if you are a seasoned manager, reviewing and exploring the various areas of management can help you refine your own management style and identify new areas for growth.

With that in mind, let's explore a simplified process for the role of a hiring manager. This process will cover key steps and strategies for successfully managing the hiring process, regardless of your level of experience.

Hiring management:

- Track current allocations of your direct reports in a visual manner. It could be a spreadsheet or an application that your organization prefers. Refer to the template available in the *Manager's Aid* GitHub repo for a sample.
- Create a forecast of your demand for at least a quarter ahead. Work with the project managers and other stakeholders in the company to accurately predict the demand. Even after that you would find yourself in ad hoc demand for developers in projects so, have some margin of buffer in your developers forecast.
- Understand the HR hiring process and common practice/norms in your organization. Those are the boundary that you shouldn't cross. Otherwise, you would find yourself in unnecessary clash with the establishments. That doesn't help you progressing your career in that organization.

Hiring steps:

- Work with the recruiting team (usually called Talent Acquisition team) to plan the hiring steps. Create an interview panel with diversified skills- technical and leadership.
- Have objective status and review status for each interviewer to provide objective feedback. Example statuses are: *Yes, No, Strongly Yes, Strongly No*.
- Create a set of questionnaires to cover the aspects: Technology, Behavioral (e.g., self-driven, challenge taker, independent, learning mindset, etc.), Communication, Culture fit, etc.
- Accumulate the panel's feedback to make the hiring decision. This can be done virtually through your company's recruiting system.

Regardless, it's better practice to have a quick call to go over each of the interviewer's summary thoughts to finalize the decision. Always make the decision using the objective criteria that you had created upfront and communicate it to the interview panel, if necessary.

- Finally, use the HR process that your company follows. Most of the time, the HR manager isn't involved in decision making apart from initial screening but better to know the company process and follow it.
- Formalize the welcoming of a new member to the team and plan a 30-60-90-Day goals and check-in. Use the template available in the *Manager's Aid* GitHub repo.

Budgeting and Forecasting

There are two main types of budgeting: (a) managing a given budget, and (b) forecasting and determining the budget needed to achieve the deliverables.

As a manager, you may find yourself engaged in either or both types of budgeting, depending on your level of involvement in the financial aspects of your team or project. Regardless of the type of budgeting you are doing, it is crucial to have a solid understanding of the financial aspects and to effectively manage the budget.

To manage a budget effectively, the first step is to account for costs. While you don't need an accounting degree to manage a budget, it is important to have a basic understanding of costing principles.

Costing is comprised of two main parts: Direct Costs and Indirect Costs. Direct Costs are tangible expenses that can be easily identified, such as hourly rates for software engineers, software license costs, hardware (e.g., laptops, servers, storage), and third-party vendor or consultant fees. To effectively manage your budget, it's essential to create a spreadsheet that itemizes each cost and its corresponding rate. It's important to be granular in your cost accounting, as lump sum accounting can lead to inefficiency and the potential for mismanagement. Use the template available in the *Manager's Aid* GitHub repo.

As a manager, you will often need to negotiate for resources from your company. To do this effectively, you must be able to present different scenarios for resourcing and their associated costs to your senior management. By having a detailed breakdown of direct costs, you can provide your management team with a comprehensive view of your budget and make informed decisions.

To make the most of your resources and ensure successful project outcomes, it's critical to have a clear understanding of your direct costs and the corresponding rates.

Indirect costs are typically overhead expenses that are not exclusively tied to your project or team but are incurred by the enterprise you work in. Examples of indirect costs include utility costs, real estate costs, inflation adjustments, company bonuses, and so on. While software development managers are usually not responsible for managing these costs, it's still important to be aware of them and track them at a high-level.

Once you have a clear understanding of the underlying costs of your project, it's important to factor in risk to manage any uncertainties. As organizational changes are inevitable, such as budget cuts due to financial situations or broader economic trends, it's crucial to include a contingency in your budget. To do this, you should engage in strategic costing by considering the variability of costs and adding a cushion to the rates of people and resources. Explicitly adding a rainy-day fund of around 10% (or whatever your organization is comfortable with) to your overall cost can help you manage any unforeseen circumstances that may arise.

It's important to note that your contingency cost may be the first to be cut by your senior management. However, by creating a contingency plan, you'll be more conscious of spending and motivated to save money to counteract the absence of a rainy-day fund. Additionally, this exercise demonstrates your management maturity to senior management and makes them aware that you're managing your project responsibly. As a result, they'll be more willing to extend support when you face financial challenges in the future.

Creating Team

As a current-day manager, one of the most important skills to hone is the ability to create and manage a team. Before delving into what a team is, it's essential to understand what it is not. When a group of individuals work together, they are simply a "group" who share resources and may be close in proximity to each other (whether physically or virtually). However, their outcomes are not necessarily tied to each other's accomplishments. This is what sets a group of people apart from a true team.

In today's work environment, managing a team is the most prevalent scenario, particularly in software development. As a Software Development Manager (SDM), it is essential to know how to create and manage a team effectively right from the start. This involves not only bringing individuals together but also inspiring them to work collaboratively towards a shared goal. By doing so, you can harness each team member's unique strengths and expertise to achieve exceptional results that are greater than the sum of their parts.

Team is defined as "... an interdependent collection of individuals who share responsibility for specific outcomes for their organization. Not everyone who works together or is in physical proximity belongs to a team. A team is a group of people who are interdependent with respect to information, resources, and skills and who seek to combine their efforts to achieve a common goal."[18]. I would simplify it as "a group of people working towards a common goal(s) where one's success or failure positively or negatively affects the outcome of that group."

Creating a team involves building and managing a group of individuals to achieve a common goal. This process includes stages of team formation, such as forming, storming, norming, and performing. Key factors in building an effective team include clear communication, building trust, creating a shared purpose, holding team members accountable, and providing feedback for continuous improvement.

Building team

Defining the goals or objectives of a team is essential for effective project management. The process of setting team goals is similar to that of defining project goals (as discussed in Chapter-4 of *Software Project Management*).

The goals of a team could be to develop a new software product, provide ongoing maintenance or enhancement of an existing software product, implement a specific software project for a customer, upgrade or re-architect a legacy software application with new technologies, such as transitioning from a monolithic to a microservices architecture, or migrate a software to a different technology infrastructure, such as from on-premise to cloud. Whatever the reason for building the team, it is important to define the goals at the beginning of the project.

While it is possible that the goals may change in the future, it is still important to set the initial goal to acknowledge the project's initial intent. If changes occur, the team can reassess and react to them accordingly. By setting clear goals from the outset, team members are more likely to be aligned and focused on achieving the desired outcomes.

To achieve the defined goals of a software project, it is important to identify the required skills and number of team members. For example, if the goal is to develop a new software product on a Java based platform, the necessary skills may include Java, React, SQL, graphics web design, user experience (UX) design, and test automation using frameworks such as Selenium. DevOps skills may also be required, such as knowledge of Kubernetes, Jenkins, Tomcat, and AWS services.

Based on these skills, the team composition could include a Technical Lead (1), Full Stack Software Engineers (3), SQA Engineers (2), a Business Analyst (1), a UX Engineer (1), a DevOps Engineer (1), a Project Manager and/or Scrum Master (0.5), and a Product Owner (1), among others.

It is important to note that the exact number of team members and their roles may vary depending on the size and complexity of the project, as well as other factors such as timelines and budget constraints. Therefore, it is crucial to carefully assess the project requirements before finalizing the team composition.

Chapter 1: Software Development Manager

Stages in Building a Team

Forming
Team acquaints and establishes ground rules. Formalities are preserved and members are treated as strangers.

Storming
Members start to communicate their feelings but still view themselves as individuals rather than part of the team. They resist control by group leaders and show hostility.

Norming
People feel part of the team and realize that they can achieve work if they accept other viewpoints.

Performing
The team works in an open and trusting atmosphere where flexibility is the key and hierarchy is of little importance.

Adjourning
The team conducts an assessment of the year and implements a plan for transitioning roles and recognizing members' contributions.

Figure-3: Stages of team building: Forming, Storming, Norming, Performing, Adjourning[1]

The five stages of team building are Forming, Storming, Norming, Performing, and Adjourning. Every team, regardless of the project's purpose, inventively goes through these stages. While these stages are a natural progression, it's important to minimize the Storming and Norming stages to ensure a more robust and long-lasting Performing stage. How do you achieve that? Here's one method for achieving this:

- Once you form the team, set them towards building the working software. Avoid staying in analysis paralysis mode even for a day.

Do not set the team free for "cultural acclamation" without a clear deliverable milestone. Otherwise, the team would start spending their time to finetune the culture in a vacuum of concrete deliverable and you would have prolonged storming and norming stages that you want to desperately shorten. ⚠

Further reading: in my opinion, there can't be a better book than this one for creating and building team:

Making the Team A Guide for Managers by *Leigh L. Thompson (5th Edition)* available on *https://www.amazon.com/dp/0132968088*

Managing the SDLC

As a manager, it is important to have expertise in Systems Development Life Cycle (SDLC). If you come from a software development background, you are expected to have experience with at least one popular SDLC methodology. However, as a manager, it is crucial to understand the pros and cons of different SDLC methods and to find the best fit for your team and projects. It is worth noting that SDLC is part of the larger project management process, with project management being the overarching framework. In subsequent chapters, I will cover both software project management and SDLC in more detail, including the nitty-gritty details of efficiently managing a software development project. There are two chapters specifically dedicated to SDLC: "*Software Development Methodology*" and "*Deep Dive into Agile.*" These chapters cover various SDLC methodologies, including the popular Scrum methodology.

Performance Management

If a manager's total span of work is painted on a canvas, performance management (individual and team) may take the largest real-estate in that picture. Most of the people-skills acquired by a manager would be at play to successfully manage this area. Keeping that importance in mind, let's understand the performance management, its goal and the mechanics of doing it effectively.

Performance Management, as the name sounds, is to plan, execute, monitor, and control the dynamics of your organization so that you can achieve the optimal outcome through the efficient use of the available resources and achieve the desired goal of project deliverables. If this may sound very academic to you, performance management in simple terms is your ability as a manager to get the best out of your people.

Goal of performance management: In a broader sense, your goal as a software development manager is to deliver a high-quality software product, which is also the ultimate goal of your performance management process. However, the performance management process has its specific goals as a sub-process. By being aware of these goals, you can measure the outcome of the process at every stage.

- Identify the strengths and weaknesses of your organization's individual members so that you can tap to those traits to effectively deliver your software deliverables.
- Create an environment of motivation where everyone would exactly know what are the expectations in the organization to grow their career and get rewarded. This will significantly reduce the subjectivity out of the calculus thus increasing trust in the process.
- Ensure the reward management is transparent to the recipients of the reward in your organization.
- Help the individuals to improve their skills through a well-structured career development process.
- Determine the bad actors in your organization early enough to minimize the toxic impact in the teams. Bad actors don't just drag the team down through their ineffectiveness but they also, actively or passively, spread the bad behavior. ⚠

Mechanics

- Start with assessing their strengths and weaknesses. They can self-asses their strengths and weakness and then you do a review of that. You may categorize them into areas of your interest in the organization. For example, Technical Skills, People Skills, Organization Skills, Managerial Skills, Career goals, etc. Use those skills to create a career development plan.
- The Career Development Plan should have SMART (Specific, Measurable, Achievable, Relevant and Time bound) goals. Set the goals with collaboration with them for each of the categories. Have a balanced mix of the skills in those categories.
- Periodically review the goals to check if they are on track to meeting those. Change or modify them if required while keeping the history of the baseline goals for future reference.
- Quantify the performance achievement at the annual (or whatever the performance management cycle in your company) review event. Reward them proportionate to their achievement and make sure to explicitly correlate those to the reward. If the performance is consistently

negative (use your own threshold of tolerance) then it should trigger the process of termination of the employee (see *Firing Management*).

Motivating your team is crucial for achieving success. However, it's important to note that not everyone is motivated by the same thing. As a manager, you should determine what motivates each team member individually and use that as a lever to pull. More details on how to motivate individual team members can be found in the "People Skills of a Manager" chapter.

To ensure a comprehensive reward system, consider including monetary rewards, promotions in the career ladder, changes in role and title, expanded roles and responsibilities, and publicly or privately recognizing their achievements based on what works best for the individual.

Team performance

It may sound obvious that team performance management should be different from managing individual performance but if you don't understand the dynamics of the team performance and master the nitty-gritty mechanics to manage teams' performance, you would find yourself bending over backward to apply the individual performance skills into it and achieve less than optimal outcomes. I am assuming you have read the "Creating and Building Team" section. If not, I would suggest covering that first. What makes the team performance management different? Team performance is like a vector in physics, the individual performance and attitude of every team member adds up or multiplies through a different equation than that of an individual. Few phenomena of team performance:

- Consider a team as an entity, similar to an individual, for which the dynamics of performance needs to be managed as one complex system.
- Team has enormous benefit to accomplish the objective however, team creates a vulnerability in performance at the time of negative individual performance.
- Individual attitude can be infectious both positively and negatively, but their impact is not equivalent. A positive attitude from every team member influences the team linearly and adds up, whereas a negative attitude from a single team member can exponentially degrade team

motivation. If **P** is the performance of a team with **m** members and **n** demotivated members, then the team's performance can be calculated as follows. A higher value of P represents a higher-performing team.

$$P = \frac{m-n}{m^n}$$

Mechanics

- To objectively evaluate team performance, you should establish metrics that align with the team's objectives and culture. You can collect data through various methods, such as one-on-one discussions with team members, surveys, or automated tools. Some examples of metrics that you can use are:
    o Timeliness and quality of deliverables, which indicate the team's efficiency and effectiveness in meeting the requirements and standards of stakeholders.
    o Team's brand value through Net Promoter Score (NPS), which reflects the satisfaction and loyalty of the team's customers or users.
    o Number and severity of conflicts within team members, which signal the level of collaboration and communication among team members.
    o Trust-based collaboration, such as the frequency and effectiveness of knowledge sharing, problem-solving, and mutual support during challenging situations.
- Reward and recognition are the cornerstone to creating a high-performing team. If team members do not receive recognition for their performance, the team will eventually disintegrate. Therefore, it is important to reward and recognize the team for their accomplishments. Details on how to reward and motivate individual team members can be found in the "*People Skills of a Manager*" chapter. A comprehensive reward system should cover a range of incentives, such as monetary rewards, career advancement, expanded roles and responsibilities, public or private recognition, and more.
- The Morale of the team is heavily influenced by a single bad Apple. So, you would have to always actively detect such individuals and

quarantine them immediately. This is something that you don't want to wait for a moment.
- Meet periodically with individuals for one-on-one meetings to get a pulse check of each member that you would need to accumulate into the team's pulse.
- Periodically review the mix of the team's dynamics. When you see the team dynamics is showing some sign of wear-and-tear, rejuvenate the team through shuffling team members internally or externally as required.
- Keep the team in a high-performing mode at all times. Similar to Newton's first law, an object will remain at rest or in uniform motion in a straight line unless acted upon by an external force. In this case, you have to keep the team in motion and constantly exert effort to maintain their momentum, as friction can slow them down.

Individual performance

To keep developers motivated and engaged, it's important to provide periodic rewards and recognition. There are various forms of recognition and rewards to cater to different behavioral aspects. For example, some people may be motivated by financial rewards, some by a change in title or increased responsibility, and others by taking ownership of new technologies or applications. It's important to find the right balance between individual rewards and maintaining a collaborative team environment. The next section covers a comprehensive mechanism for rewarding and recognizing individuals.

Reward and Recognition

This is the fuel that keeps an individual and a team striving to accomplish the objectives and become a high-performer. As a manager your effectiveness is measured through timely recognition of the high-performing individuals and teams and reward them.

Here are few popular reward tools that you can use for individual performance recognition:

- Financial rewards: This could be in the form of bonuses, stock options, or profit sharing.
- Promotions: This could be a change in title, added responsibilities, or a new job position.
- Public recognition: This could be through an internal newsletter, company-wide email, or announcement at a team meeting.
- Private recognition: This could be a one-on-one meeting with the manager or a personalized note of appreciation.
- Opportunities for skill development: This could be through attending conferences, training sessions, or mentoring opportunities.
- Flexible work arrangements: This could be through the option to work from home or flexible hours.

However, it's important to note that rewards and recognition can also create unintended competition and negatively impact team dynamics if not managed carefully. To avoid this, a delicate balance must be maintained between rewarding individuals and upholding team spirit and collaboration. Here is a sample framework for rewards and recognition:

- Make the recognition process as transparent as possible. Lack of transparency will turn your best honest initiative much less effective if not outright controversial.
- Get feedback from customers, team lead, team members and use that as the basis for recognition.
- Recognition can be either public recognition with reward or private recognition reward or both. Not everyone likes it to be public so use it wisely depending on the individual's motivational trigger point. The public option should have Social Networking (LinkedIn) integration as well.

In addition to top-down reward and recognition, allow anyone to nominate others for recognition through the gamification of the process. This will democratize the process and balance with the collaborative environment. Use a tool that makes it easy and fun to democratize the recognition/reward. If the process is too cumbersome and clunky, it won't last for long.

Below is a sample depiction of a reward system:
- Individuals would have a credit pool from which they can recognize others and award reward points.
- The reward points should be convertible to dollars (e.g., 10 pts = $1) or company internal perks (e.g., 2,000 pts = 1 Paid Time Off or PTO).
- Manager approval can be added to the process, but it could create bureaucracy, which may become counterproductive to the goal of the reward process. So, depending on your level of confidence in the organization, you can add that level of bureaucracy for a time being.

By implementing a comprehensive and thoughtful rewards and recognition framework, managers can keep their developers motivated and engaged while also maintaining a collaborative team environment.

Firing

One of the most challenging aspects of management is terminating team members. While hiring is an essential part of a manager's role, firing can be equally crucial. Unfortunately, it's a neglected and often disliked part of management, as nobody likes to be the "bad guy" associated with negative actions.

Firing Management

Even if it may sound like another task in the management process, but mark my word, this is the task that you don't want to do without knowing it very well. This may not only be the costliest decision you make in your management role but this may very well become a legal quagmire for the HR in your company, if not for you directly. Especially, if you consider it as a power to show that you are a manager and in charge of someone else's employment, you need to first cool down a bit and understand the cost of it. Most of the time Firing is the result of the "bug" in the hiring process. In some cases, you would have to take that action for someone else's bad hiring decision in the past. So, when you're at the point of firing someone, you and your organization have most probably already incurred some loss due to the lack of skill or unaccepted behavioral issue that triggers the termination. However, remember that if you don't decide decisively

Chapter 1: Software Development Manager

sooner (refer to Effective Decision Making in the chapter: People Skills of a Manager) then you may continue to accumulate not only the loss for your organization but you also ruin the career of that employee who should get a chance to fix their career and may be in a different organization. ⚠

Follow the below process to effectively handle the termination process:

- Regardless of whatever firing management process you use, you should always use the 360-degree feedback to continuously monitor your direct reports and keep the outcome documented. ⚠
- If there's a situation where an immediate fireable offense is made where you can't wait to initiate the process, then you are short-circuited to the termination immediately and just clean up the mess afterwards.

However, if you need to initiate the termination process due to ongoing performance or behavioral reason, then follow these steps:

- First, understand the company policy on employee termination. Your company may have unique policies and procedures in place along with industry-standard management practices. You have to work within the boundaries of those rules.
- The goal of this process is not to reach the point of termination. This process should be implemented in such a way that it gives the employee a fair chance to achieve the targeted performance level and continue in the organization or demonstrate concrete progress and accomplish the target performance goals, failing which, due process for termination will be followed.
- Create a concrete set of objectives in writing with clear expectations of the next improvement goals.
- Meet with the individual to kick off the process by explaining the reason why this process has been initiated, how it will benefit both the individual and the organization. This is very critical to demonstrate that this is a win-win process, and both parties will benefit at the end.
- Schedule periodic meetings to review the progress and provide feedback on the progress. This should be documented in writing. ⚠

Based on the outcome of the progress, make the decision. If the employee rebounds and achieves the desired performance, then the process ends with returning to business-as-usual. On the contrary outcome, where the set targets aren't met, initiate the firing process, work with HR and ensure that everything goes according to your Company's HR and code-of-conduct Policies. Note that terminating an employee is a serious decision that requires careful consideration and adherence to company policies and procedures. If you are unsure or need guidance, seek advice from your HR department or higher management.

CHAPTER II

Chapter 2: Manager as a Leader

Leadership is a crucial trait that distinguishes a manager in their role. While it is possible to be a manager without being a leader, this can be challenging, particularly in the software development field. John Kotter's[22] definition of management and leadership is especially relevant in this context: "Management focuses on creating order through processes, whereas leadership focuses on creating change through a vision." However, becoming proficient in leadership may take time and experience. Nevertheless, understanding this concept is essential for effective technology leadership. It can also differentiate you from a mediocre manager who can manage day-to-day development but cannot contribute to the company's future growth.

Technology Leadership

As a technology leader you will not only be expected to run the ongoing development but also to contribute in the road-mapping for the company. Usually, the senior level leadership is involved in creating the roadmap. It doesn't harm, rather I would argue that it would be helpful for your career to understand the process. Nonetheless, in the end, you or the likes of you, the managers, would be on the ground implementing those strategic leadership decisions.

Every organization has to have their long-term vision to where the company targets to reach. Technology plays a significant role in it. So, the Technology roadmap would be a big part of the company roadmap. A technology leader is always aware of the company vision and the future trend of the technological landscape. Based on that the company roadmap should be created. Here are few things that you should know about technology road-mapping:

- Technology Roadmap is done usually for 1-3 years with short term and medium-term milestones to achieve.
- Review the current product and technology stacks used in the organizations, propose to invest more into those areas if these are aligned with the company vision and future technology trend. If gaps are found in that assessment, then a transformational program should

be proposed to bring new technology stack and build new software products to close the gap.
- Process improvement is a big area that sometimes gets shadowed by the technology roadmap. For example, do you continue to use Agile methodology for the project team, IT and Business alike?
- People and their skills are to be aligned towards the direction the company is heading. Do you need more traditional developers? Are you going into Artificial Intelligence based solutions in the future? What skills the current developers have and what they need to acquire to stay relevant in the future organization?
- There would have to be a program to either retrain the existing workforce or adjust the workforce to realign to reach the roadmap target.

Strategic Leadership

Strategic leadership is a higher level of leadership that entails the capacity to think and act strategically towards the goals and objectives of the organization. If you can, always try to contribute to the company's strategy and vision. What can you do to contribute to the company's strategic roadmap?

- Be part of the group who would be developing the roadmap. If you are capable enough, initiate the creation of a roadmap. Conduct an Ideation program to get input from the relevant talents.
- Get buy-in from the executive leadership in the company. These kind of initiative needs significant company resources, so without a strong buy-in you will never be able to achieve your roadmap goal.
- Make sure to understand the stakeholders in the company. There would be certain stakeholders who would be crucial to come up with a strategic roadmap. They would also be critical to successfully execute the roadmap plan. Similarly, there may be stakeholders who are not aligned with your roadmap initiative and may attempt to hinder its success. There could be legitimate reasons behind that or sometimes just

human ego. Nonetheless, you would have to tackle all those forces for a successful futuristic roadmap and execution.
- Iteratively create the roadmap: create the first version as draft, review with the trusted leadership group to get their feedback, incorporate the feedback, refine it and then finalize it.
- Once finalized, present the roadmap to the organization's leadership and decision makers. It is important that you have to conduct a "marketing" campaign to sell your roadmap to everyone who would be impacted positively or negatively by the execution of the roadmap. Except for a very few- no one likes "change". So, you have to be a change leader, championing your proposed changes by showing the values this roadmap would bring to the company and how this would help them for a strong future.

I have just scratched the surface of this strategic leadership role because you won't be expected to do this for the first few years of your journey in the Software Development Management. So, feel free to ignore for now what I just mentioned above and continue to play your daily management role if you think it's not your cup of tea at this stage of your career.

PART II
People *aspects of* Management

CHAPTER III

Chapter 3: People Skills of a Manager

These skills are pretty standard and usually have nothing to do with software development. And many times, you would learn these skills as part of your day-to-day life. However, if you aren't aware of the standardized vocabulary of those skills then you will not only be able to communicate with others effectively but it will also make your life harder and very inefficient in managing people. Furthermore, lack of these people skill "tools" would stifle your ability to measure your effectiveness and improve incrementally thereafter.

Have you seen a plumber or an electrician go to their job site without their toolbox? Never. Because without the toolbox, they cannot do their job effectively. Similarly, you as a manager need to carry the management skills "toolbox", if you will, always with you to perform your day-to-day job at your work. These skills are like the variety of tools in your toolbox. If you haven't built your "management toolbox" yet, no worries at all. Luckily you can create this toolbox by training your brain "muscles". I will walk you through each of the skills and how to use them so that you won't be unprepared at your job site.

Additionally, you need to learn when to use what tool. For example, when you need screws to be fastened then you certainly would have to use a screwdriver or if you need to create a hole in the wall, you will take out the drill from your toolbox. If you start using a hammer instead of a drill to make a hole in the wall then you won't just create a mess but you would be miserably inefficient in managing teams. Hence, I'll try to show you each of the tools in a simulated fashion to find the best matched tool in your day-to-day work from the perspective of a software development manager.

Critical Thinking

Critical Thinking is defined by the Oxford dictionary as "the objective analysis and evaluation of an issue in order to form a judgment." This definition encapsulates the essence of what it means to be a manager. As a manager, you are responsible for solving problems every day through decisive judgment. However, the problems you are tasked with solving involve people and technology, which makes them unique. The subjective nature of human thought processes combined with the objective nature of technology requires you to rise above subjectivity and evaluate situations objectively. Therefore, it is crucial to develop your critical thinking skills as a manager.

Here are the few techniques that you can use to be a critical thinker:

- When you are given a situation, blur out the person from the situation. If that's too difficult for you then you can replace that person by yourself i.e., put yourself in their shoes. In human psychology this is called *Empathy* or *Second-level thinking*.
- Understand the environment and the surroundings of the situation to get the full context of the situation.
- Asking questions is a key way to explore a topic and understand it more deeply. Try to ask open-ended questions that require more than a "yes" or "no" answer.
- Never rely on one source of information to avoid biases. Use Triangulation technique by using multiple credible sources of information to enrich your thinking and decision making. Be open to consider different viewpoints and arguments.
- Once you have gathered information, carefully consider the evidence and arguments being presented. Look for logical flaws or gaps in the reasoning, and consider whether the evidence supports the claims being made.
- It's important to be aware of your own biases and assumptions, as they can influence your thinking. Try to be open-minded and consider multiple perspectives.

Effective Decision Making

Effective Decision Making is the process by which you can make the most efficient decision for you and your team, taking into account all the factors at hand including the time and place. This skill sets apart leaders from followers in the organization, as the ability to make effective and timely decisions is key to success. While there's no one-size-fits-all method for making decisions, here's a simple framework that you can train yourself to utilize:

- Define the problem: Before you can make a decision, you need to understand what the problem is. Take the time to define the problem, identify the root cause, and gather all relevant information.
- Analyze the situation: Once you understand the problem, take the time to analyze the situation. Consider the pros and cons of each potential decision, and evaluate the potential outcomes.
- Consider your options: Think creatively and come up with a range of potential solutions to the problem. Evaluate each option and consider the impact it will have on your team, organization, and stakeholders.
- Seek input from others: Don't make decisions in a vacuum. Seek input and feedback from other team members, stakeholders, and subject matter experts.
- Make a decision and take action: Once you've evaluated your options and gathered input, make a decision and take action. Be decisive and follow through on your decision.
- Evaluate the results: After taking action, evaluate the results and adjust your approach as necessary. Learn from your decision-making process and use that knowledge to improve your skills going forward.

In addition to the simple framework mentioned above, there are four high-level decision-making strategies that you should be aware of and confident in practicing if your job function requires them.

Data driven decision making

This is the most effective, least confrontational, and repeatable way of decision making. Gather data points and statistics of the situation. Create a forecast based on those data points. e.g., imagine you want to create a backup storage solution and would like to determine which storage system you want to choose for that. Gather the current size of data, growth curve of last X years, projection of the data growth for next Y years. Then compare the cost of each storage system and performance metrics based on the growth projection and present your decisions.

Intuition driven decision making

Intuition is defined by Oxford Language as "the ability to understand something immediately, without the need for conscious reasoning." This is also synonymous with the word "instinct". This clearly tells us that intuition is related and tied to our physiological nature as humans. This skill was gradually built for thousands if not millions of years through our evolution as humans. I would also argue that this is the most advanced attribute we're born with and made us who we are today. We use this in our daily life at every moment without even realizing it. The question is how do you use this highly sophisticated tool effectively in the field of management and leadership. Because the intuition that we are ingrained with and build everyday isn't for the software development field. So, if you apply your intuition from farming or hunting as-is to software development then you're shooting yourself in the foot. So, the first step of this would be to build your intuition in software development (it's true for all other faculty but this book is for the software development manager so I am confining this to that alone). ⚠

Intuition (or colloquially known as "gut feelings") sounds so unprofessional that most management books won't even mention it at all. They would consider this as voodoo or fortune telling. I won't blame them fully for that as well. Let me first clear up some doubts that you will hear from many traditional managers:

"Intuition is like religious belief where you say that you just believe but you can't explain what are the basis of your belief or the rationale behind that. Neither you are ready to put that to a rational test nor would you be ready to accept an alternative if you cannot be convinced otherwise."

If you use intuition in that manner, yes, I would suggest you skip this section and pretend you never heard of it. As you are still continuing with this section that means you are a rational person and ready to experiment with your decision-making process.

Prerequisite to intuition driven decision making:

- You have been in the similar field of industry and/or domain for at least 10 years or equivalent. The equivalency would be like you were a key part of development and delivery of at least 3 to 5 large projects or initiatives. Never delude yourself after your 2nd large projects or initiatives pretending that you have built your intuition skills: Yes, you now have enough knowledge to make knowledge-based decisions but you haven't built necessary wisdom to it which is the foundation to intuition-driven decision making.
- You are a rational person. Emotion is necessary to be a human but if your rationality can't supersede your emotionality, then you would fall into the trap of an arrogant leader rather than an effective leader. How do you know you're a rational leader? You can accept your failure of your decision by overriding your ego and be able to course correct immediately after your intuition is proved wrong. If you can't accept that at times you can be wrong, then institution shouldn't be the tool in your leadership toolbox.

With that prerequisite, now you're ready to build this skill. Follow these steps:

- Assess the situation in which you are going to make the decision. Don't fall into the trap that this is just another software development project or initiative. Every initiative is different because the people who worked with, the technology you used or were available, and the customers that you interacted with all are different. In terms of people, even if they are the same people but they are different at least in their level of experiences. For instance, if the developers were the same people that had worked with you in that project but they are now a one-more-project-experienced compare to the last one. If the technology stack for the project is the same for the current project, then that's a bigger problem that you should solve first- using the older technologies in your new project shows that you're falling behind in using the latest updated tech stack. In every 6-12 months (or in every 2 years, if you are a believer in Moore's Law) the technology landscape shifts towards the future.

- Do a gap analysis of the internal and external factors (budget, sponsors, skills of the developers, customers knowledge base and their sophistication level, etc.) and create a map to bridge the gap. You can put that on paper or in your head depending on the extent of the decision you are going to make.
- Come up with at least two alternative decisions that you can apply. If you can't come up with any alternative approach or decisions, then it's a sign that you didn't build enough experience to effectively and confidently make intuitive decisions. Evaluate the alternate decisions and pick the one that you intuitively are more inclined to. Trust your intuition (as you're in the decision-making process, the expectation is you've created enough wisdom to differentiate between Intuition and wild-guess).
- Constantly gather feedback and monitor the outcome of your decision. Be prepared to tweak and tune it as you see signs of ineffectiveness.

Hybrid decision making

As the word says it all: use both Data driven and Intuition driven approaches to nail the decision. This is very effective when you haven't built your rapport or brand image as a successful leader (or you don't have a proven track record in the organization) as your intuition would be somewhat backed up by the metrics used to create that intuition. Below are some best practices:

- Understand the problem in detail by talking to the people who are influencing or being impacted by your decision. Use *Critical Thinking* skill to analyze it critically.
- Come up with alternate options with corresponding pros and cons. No decision is perfect – you just pick the best alternative at that point in time.
- Build relationships and rapport with the stakeholders and who can influence to implement your decision. Sometimes it's called "pre-meeting influence" to decision making. There's a saying that advises against declaring your decision in a meeting like dropping a bombshell, as even if your decision is the most accurate one, it may still provoke

immediate backlash. Additionally, if you are to brainstorm for a decision, don't get to the meeting without some sort of pre-meeting discussion to have a pulse-check of the participants. At the very least give them heads-up on your thought process. Nobody likes to be surprised even if that goes along with their thought process. That's more of psychology (like prestige, ego, perceived image, etc.) rather than physics.

- Be dynamic and review the outcome of your decision. Be prepared to tweak it as needed. The last thing you want to do is to be emotionally attached to your decision. that's easy to say but harder to achieve. Detach yourself from the decision itself. That's the only thing, the objective decision that you can objectively discuss with others.
- You own the decision's outcome so take the responsibility of the outcome. That means you take the credit for the success-outcome of your decision as well as own the responsibilities of the failure-outcome of the decision. There would be an unwritten threshold (each organization and industry have their own thresholds based on its culture) that would define how much and how many failures you can have in a certain time window.
- Be mindful that you wouldn't be right all the time. In fact, statistically speaking, you would be wrong quite often. Your effectiveness as a leader would be how small the negative impact of the decision remains and how quickly you can course correct and come up with the next right decision.

Ethical decision making

This is another skill that you need to learn to have a successful long career. You may achieve short term success and grow quickly through unethical decision making but you would find yourself in a mess like spider wave if not in a legal quagmire and shortened your successful career.

Use the below techniques to make ethical decision making. Ask yourself about the situation and the decision:

- Is this within the boundary of legal systems?
- Is this within the boundary of social and moral accepted notions

- What would you feel if it was done to you?
- Are you okay with everyone surrounding you doing this in your organization and society?

If answers to any of the above questions is no, then rethink the decision you made.

So far, I have discussed how to effectively make decisions. However, there's another aspect of decision making which is to influence others to get the necessary buy-in to move the needle. Suppose you're going into a meeting to declare a newly made decision. If you go into the meeting and share your decision like a bomb-shell dropped during the meeting, then the chance is very high that you will face opposition or at the very least resistance from the very people who supposed to be benefitted from that decision. You would also need many people on your side to effectively execute your decision. You can try a technique called *Pre-announcement Influence* to decision making where you get the buy-in to your decision preemptively. ⚠

You can use the below technique:

- Determine the stakeholders who would be impacted by the decision: positively or negatively.
- Identify the people who would have influence to the larger group or to the entire organization.
- Meet with those influencers as early as possible to get their opinion. Share your directions of thought. Be prepared to tweak your decision based on their feedback. It's very important to get buy-in from those influencers.
- Meet with other members "unofficially" or "casually" to give them heads up on what's coming.
- Once you are positive about the stakeholder's reaction and their appetite to the decision's action items, then you can go for formal announcement of the decision.
- Sometimes you may skip such "pre-announcement influencing" if you've built the branding of your image in such a way that you have a

high level of respect and authority. However, do not keep surprising them at all the time as this may diminish your influence if used repeatedly done.

Motivating

Oxford language defines "Motivate" as "stimulate (someone's) interest in or enthusiasm for doing something." As a manager, your job is to motivate every member in your organization to achieve the set objectives in the team. Through the motivating process the expected outcome is to move the individuals into the state of "being motivated" state where they can accomplish more than they thought they were able to.

This is the soft power that is like the salt to a chef, if you will, that you would need to use everywhere and every day at your workplace. You need to use it wisely - if you use it less than needed then you would find a less than optimal employee base in your organization. However, if you use it more, then you would find yourself in the group of hyped up over-stimulated employees who are detached to reality.

Why to motivate?

- Motivated people are good to work with. We spend a third of our day, at least, at our work. You don't want to be around demotivated people to have your personal well-being.
- Motivated people accomplish their tasks much faster and efficiently compared to non-motivated personnel.
- It's very hard and costly to manage a demotivated employee.
- Demotivated people are toxic and they not only stay in the state of demotivation but pull other people into the spiral of their demotivation zone.

Mechanics

- Observe and listen to your team who you are going to motivate them.
- Use *Empathy* (also known as *Emotional IQ* or *Second Level Thinking*) to put yourself into their shoes: what would motivate you if you were them.

- Create a complete plan to motivate them. This would include-
  o Verbalizing the commitments.
  o Execute the plan to materialize the benefits.
  o Monitor the effectiveness to see if your plan is improving the motivation of your team.
  o Tune, tweak or course correct as needed to make it more effective.

Effective Communication

One of my professors during my MBA program, jokingly said that the word "communication" is in essence plural even though the dictionary would tell you that it's singular. His funny argument was "you can't have communication without two parties involved in it, the sender and receiver". Anyone can do the communication part in any form and manner but the goal is to turn that into effective communication i.e., to achieve the goal that you want to achieve through your communication. I feel compelled to say that the leadership of a manager is as good as their effectiveness in communication.

Communication primarily has two forms: Verbal and Written. Verbal (and in-person) communication has more impact to positively influence than written communication. Apart from written communication's shortcomings due to the inherent nature of duality (or plurality) in meaning but not able to convey the feeling of the sender which is especially true in a formal communication setting. So, make sure the verbal, face-to-face communication is always in the mix of every communication you do. It is always the right mix of verbal and written communication that makes the communication effective. At the minimum, initiate the communication using verbal form and then subsequently use written communication (like email, memo, chat conversation, etc.). However, if you use email or chat, do not let that beyond a few replies (you pick the threshold but 3-5 follow up probably where you want to cut the writing and get back to in-person). ⚠

Use written communication as a companion to verbal or face-to-face communication. Use it as the sole communication channel where there's a physical barrier to use face-to-face where it's practically impossible.

Always summarize your discussion points and send them to the participants to be on the same page. This would save you from future scenarios where you thought you conveyed everyone's agreement or disagreement of something but later you would be surprised by how many times your assumptions prove to be incorrect.

Though this may well fall under a separate skill title but I am putting this under communication as you do not need to excel at it to be an effective manager but the more you have that skill it's easier for you to be an effective manager and leader - which is public speaking. Toastmaster is a great organization that you can join if you think you lack public speaking or are afraid of speaking in public.

Effective Negotiation

Negotiation is not specific to a manager's skill, rather it's a generic skill that everyone uses to their day-to-day life, such as, when you had planned your last vacation, you have already used negotiation skill with your friend or family members to pick the vacation destination. So, it's not something new to you. However, as a manager, you have to use negotiation effectively to achieve a wide variety of objectives, such as: budget allocation for your organization, hiring a new member and their compensation negotiation, project resource allocations, project's scope-timeline-resource management, etc. Because of the intense usage of this skill, it's important to be expert on the process of negotiation and alternate approaches to it.

Effective negotiation can be defined as: "the process of reaching an agreement with another party through a mutually beneficial exchange of ideas, resources, or needs." The most important part of that is that both of the parties involved in the negotiation should feel that the outcome was "mutually beneficial and satisfactory." Absence of that outcome isn't negotiation but forcing your opinion on others to agree. As a manager or leader at the company, you would have some authority through which you can achieve that "forced" agreement and that's the risk you carry if you don't get expertise in the negotiation skill. If you continue to "force" your opinions to others, you will end up with demotivated direct reports and lots of enemies in the organization.

Mechanics

- Preparation is key. Never walk into a negotiation without preparation. Research the issue and the other party, define the objective that you want to achieve through the negotiation and set your bottom line. The objective should have enough flexibility with a range of possible outcomes. However, be willing to walk away if the other party doesn't meet your bottom line.
- Set the stage of the negotiation. That depends on the environment but make sure to block enough time and a secure location (be it physical or a virtual conference room). Many negotiations end up to failure because you run out of time and walk out with a less than optimal outcome.
- Be objective instead of subjective. If you can take out subjectivity from the discussion that's better but if you can't, at least qualify that with an objective clause. E.g., instead of saying: "I need person X in the project", say: "I need person X in the project to achieve the project timeline".
- Use communication skills effectively. Never use negative languages in your conversation. This is true for any communication but especially critical in the negotiation discussion. Use of positive words would create a positive environment conducive to positive outcome. Also, try to use more open-ended questions when probing for detail.
- There are many negotiation tactics that you can use however make sure to use it appropriately:
  o Building relationship: building relationship is the most effective tactic to achieve desired outcome.
  o During the negotiation, you can start it by offering first (known as Anchoring) to the counterparty. This may help you to influence the final outcome.

- o BATNA (Best Alternative To a Negotiated Agreement) is the most common approach where you walk away with the best alternative outcome.
- o Finally, you can use Emotion and Power as negotiation tactics however those should be the absolute last resort as those tactics have diminishing utility if you overuse them.

Managing conflicts

The word conflict may be too "heavy" or even "negative" at times when you're just working with two individuals to find a common ground or sweet spot. The word Conflict is defined in Oxford dictionary as "a serious disagreement or argument, typically a protracted one." As the Management study uses this term, I am keeping this vocabulary but I rather use this word carefully when we go use this tool. Maybe the better wording could be "Managing discord" or something like that. Regardless of the term, let's deep dive on how you can manage conflicts (or discord).

- First principle of conflict resolution is to use the adage "offense is the best defense". The best defense mechanism is to create transparency in your organization where you don't allow one to unethically or falsely complain about others. Because many conflicts aren't actually conflicts but just complaining about one another. So, when you keep a transparent environment and be fair to all, then they try to either resolve it by themselves or even withdraw their complaints. This will also reduce future conflicts. Be aware that even if you resolve the conflict between two parties, it's like using glue to repair a broken glass - that won't be completely smooth ever. ⚠
- If you are able to bring both parties involved in the conflict onto the same table, invite both parties in a meeting, be it in person or on video conference. You often will find that even the possibility of facing the other person diminishes the very conflict. However, if the conflict doesn't go away then make sure that you don't talk to them in isolation. If you're forced to listen to one of them then make sure to tell them that you are going to have a joint meeting with both the parties.

- Let both of the parties explain their stands. Listen to them carefully (using the *Effective Listening* method).
- Put the conflict into the big picture and see how that goes along with or contradicts the company vision and goals. Use both *Effective and Ethical Decision-Making* methods to ensure that you don't take the decision in a biased way or delay the making of very decisions. Your decision should have three components: (a) Your analysis of the situation through the lens of company vision and goals in a big picture (b) Reminder on how their conflict is obstructing the accomplishment of the bigger goal, and finally (c) the decision and follow up with action items.
- Communicate your decision to both the conflicting parties using the *Constructive Feedback* method to both parties. Ask for their feedback. If they agree with your decision, well and good. Continue with a follow up meeting to repeat the above, if need be. This time you would handle the residue conflict instead of the baseline initial conflict.
- Nonetheless, have a follow up after a certain period to see if the conflict is completely resolved.

As a cautious reminder: never *delegate* the conflict resolution. This is entirely a managerial responsibility and you have to take action personally. Delegating it to someone else undermines your ability, leadership and brand image. Sometimes, you may engage your manager in this matter but it's always better if you use their authority and influence to resolve the conflict rather than delegating it to them.[2] ⚠

Effective Delegation

Delegation is one of the most important tools for a leader to become successful in their role. Most of the new leaders struggle to effectively delegate work. Delegation is not dumping work to your team members or getting rid of your work. Something you can't and shouldn't delegate. It reminds the famous Goldilocks story: you don't delegate everything; you also don't keep everything with you but you delegate that's just right for you and the team.

- Identify the work that can be delegated. Not everything can and should be delegated. Examples of non-delegate-able works are: individual performance management, top level decision making, creating your organization's mission and goals, Team building, project initiation, etc.
- Identify who is skilled to take the work. You should have a clear understanding and knowledge of individual members' strengths and weaknesses in your organization. Someone may need a clear plan of action to start with and some others may be good at just setting the goal. Someone may need close monitoring and some others may be good at self-managing and proactively reaching out to you.
- Determine the priority and urgency. Communicate clearly the goal, timelines and success criteria. This sets apart from dumping the work over effective delegation. If you aren't communicating the outcome properly, don't delegate at all. Remember that no one has any access to your brain unless you dump your brain on paper to put your expectations black and white. ⚠
- Schedule periodic check-in. Depending on the nature of the person, if they don't have a past history of delivering it on time, make it more frequent.
- Have a contingency plan. This doesn't mean that you have to have another person to back it up as that's not realistic to have two people assigned at the same work. So, what are the options?
  - If you have the capacity to do that, you can be the backup.
  - Keeping another member Informed on the work (Scrum methodology is designed for that if you use Scrum SDLC)
  - Have leverage in the deliverable in terms of time or scope – if you don't have it, create it.

Highly recommended reading material for further learning:

Harvard Business Review (HBR) Article of To Be a Great Leader You Have to Learn How to Delegate Well.

Effective Listening

Even though it sounds so simple as a skill, the impact of it goes deep. Let's first clarify how *Listening* is different from *"Effective Listening"*. When you just listen, it doesn't explicitly define the post action of the action of listening. Through effective listening, you just don't excel in listening but you use this tool effectively to produce results. It would be used in many situations that may include: group meeting, one-on-one, conflict resolution, performance review, etc.

Use these below techniques in a group setting:

- Take note of important discussion points while others are talking. You can later refer to your note when responding to them.
- Never interrupt others. This may sound tempting to make your point but wait for the right moment to respond.

Use these below techniques for individualized discussion:

- Depending on the significance of the discussion, create the environment where you can have uninterrupted listening. If the discussion is confidential, make sure to find a meeting room or a quiet space if you don't have a confined office room so that they feel safe to speak. If you use video conference calls, make sure to create a unique meeting invite that's password protected to avoid others crashing your general meeting link unintentionally.
- Set the structure of the discussion so that the person you would be listening to has a clear expectation of their time. To illustrate: if it's a 30-minute meeting, you can set the structure as 10 minutes you listen, 10 minutes you respond and 10 minutes follow through and back-and-forth.
- Allow the person to speak freely during their time. Do not interrupt for any reason whatsoever. Unless you didn't understand what are they saying at all, then you can ask to repeat but do not ask to clarify during their first conversation. Take notes. This is useful for you to be objective and correct during your response. Moreover, this gives the impression to the meeting participants that you're serious about the discussion.

- Once they finish their talk, ask clarification questions, if any, before you give your response. This helps to avoid any misunderstanding from your side. Also, it gives positive feedback to the participants about your seriousness.
- Take a moment to analyze your response. Analyze the points using critical reasoning. Use objective analysis of the facts presented to you. Remove the "person" from the discussion points. Put yourself into their shoes and try to see from their eyes. Formulate your response and present that factually.
- Act like a reductionist. Never use the example they have given as anecdotal reference rather use that scenario to create a generic situation and wrap your response around that generic situation. You can provide an anecdotal response but try to use a separate issue other than the very specific issue unless you're doing a conflict resolution of a particular issue.
- After you present your response, ask for their confirmation on their understanding. Listen carefully to make sure they got what you wanted to convey.

The above encounter would happen very quickly during your meeting with them so you would have to practice such that it becomes your second nature.

Emotional Intelligence and Second-Order thinking

These are two emotional or behavioral aspects of leadership that were finally entered in the formal management practice as well as codified to assess it. Many of you already possess it but may not have used such vocabularies for that. These are usually gained through growing up and from the society we live in however, if you are lacking those skills, that's not the end of the world. The skills can be learned to some extent and I will describe that here that you practice. So, if you aren't naturally tuned to it at least you can add those skills to overcome your shortcomings.

Oxford dictionary defines Emotional Intelligence (EI) as "the capacity to be aware of, control, and express one's emotions, and to handle interpersonal relationships judiciously and empathetically." This is to be situational aware of the surroundings, the people and their emotions in decision making.

Second-Order thinking is to understand the next level impact of any actions or events that aren't immediately visible from outset.

Mechanics

- Do not jump into the solution immediately. Ask questions to understand it from a 360-degree perspective: What triggered the situation, who triggered it, what are the immediate impacts and what are the second-level impacts that we don't see immediately. ⚠
- Use empathy: put yourself into the other person's shoes, why would you have said or done something like that? What outcome would you expect out of it?
- Make decisions based on the EI and Second-level thinking. Create a coherent connected message behind your decision so that you can convince others to justify.

Recommended reading:

https://fs.blog/second-order-thinking/
https://hbr.org/2017/02/emotional-intelligence-has-12-elements-which-do-you-need-to-work-on

Constructive Feedback Essentials

The goal of Constructive feedback is to provide both positive and negative feedback to your employee in a positive manner so that the receiver of the feedback is more susceptible to accept it thus creates a positive environment in the organization.

Prerequisite of constructive feedback:

- In person (or on video call when remote) is much more preferable than just on call. Email should be absolutely the last resort for providing constructive feedback.

- You should have a trusted relationship already built with the person who you want to give constructive feedback. Absence of trust on you, no matter what technique you apply, would be of no value whatsoever.
- Make sure you have practiced the Effective Listening skill and fully confident in that.

Once you have fulfilled the pre-requisites, follow the rest:

- Use an objective approach focusing on the issue rather than the person.
- Use the widely famous *Sandwich* approach of communication:
  - start with what you noticed about the positive thing about that person or the situation.
  - Determine and inform them what's causing the issue or holding them back to solve the situation.
  - Finally, end with a positive note by showing them the benefit of what they would achieve if they can fix the issue.
- Get confirmation that the feedback is received and accepted.

Fuel Innovation and Creativity

This particular soft skill makes Software Development management unique in comparison to many other fields. Innovation and creativity are the everyday business a software development team is engaged in. So, as a manager your role should be to spark innovation and creativity in your organization. You would find many Software Development Managers without the ability to spark innovation or creativity which is a disservice to a group of talented individuals who are capable of being creative and innovative. You wouldn't just do a disservice to themselves and yourself but also hinder their career from flourishing.

Software developers are basically and inherently creative. If they aren't creative, they wouldn't be or can't flourish in this software development business. So, in one sense it may seem like a cake walk to spark innovation and creativity to a bunch of creative folks but it's actually harder than it sounds. The challenge is that you can't tell a creative person to be creative. That just doesn't work. It's more subtle and nimble. So how would you do it?

- Do not micromanage! This is the first, second and third law and you can continue till how far you want to count. But do not micromanage, period! ⚠
- Create a healthy competition within the organization. This doesn't need to be a competition with each other all the time but it could be even within each of everyone to beat their own accomplishments.
- Show respect and give the right appreciation to the creative people. Even if you may be smarter than them, do not arrogantly show your smartness over others as you will win the battle but lose the war.
- Money is needed to live in a human society but most creative people need recognition first and then money.
- People don't earn money through creativity but their creativity brings you money. It's subtle but profound – sooner you understand it better for you to manage creativity.
- Remove the administrative and bureaucratic "red tapes". Create a support structure that keeps the road to creativity clean of any hazards.
- Set challenging and lofty goals. The creative people are usually highly ambitious and some are "egoistic" to some extent. The higher the goal is the more motivated they become to reach that high.
- Creative people are a mix of introvert and extrovert behavior. Oftentimes more introverted than not. Regardless, don't push them to one side from others. Let them flourish in their own nature and continue to be creative.

Influence Courageously

This is a skill that a traditional manager often lacks due to their obsession of using hard authority over other soft power. Also, many other disciplines don't require as much soft power as a software development team would require. Nonetheless, software development management requires less use of authority to maintain the creativity in the team as well as more use of self-organization to sustain a continuous quality delivery. In that sense achieving the same outcome through influencing is preferred over exerting authority.

Benefits

- You can avoid micromanagement. Even though in some cases (e.g., at the early stage of project initiation, or if an emergency situation arises where the stakes are too high, etc.) you have to micromanage, the cost of micromanagement is too high. It takes away all your time and energy on others than you excelling in your role. So, if you can achieve the outcome without micromanagement, that's not only less stressful but also more sustainable.
- Through influencing you can create the state of a "self-organized" team. You can continue to reap all the benefits of a self-organized team which is the best that you can achieve from a team.
- Keeping the team member motivated. Creative minds like the Software Developers usually don't like to be micromanaged.

Mechanics

- Listen to the facts, context and opinions of the team members involved in the situation. Let everyone feel they are given a fair chance to speak-up and their voices are heard.
- Ask intriguing questions to ensure all the perspectives of the issues are covered. If you feel any specific areas are left untouched, then bring those ideas to them. E.g., when you're in a system architecting meeting, wait till end if all the software quality attributes (e.g., maintainability, testability, scalability, performance, security, etc.) are considered and if not, then you can bring your thoughts that weren't covered.
- If you find the right decisions are being taken by the team, then remain as the cheerleader of the team. Don't snatch away their credits.
- When you find that the decision isn't towards the direction of your organization or doesn't meet the goals of the strategic interest, bring your ideas to the table.
- Always use three steps while presenting your ideas and decisions to the group: Company Goals, Project or Team goals, outcome that matters to the customers of the systems being developed. Keeping the big picture of the organization is the natural influencer.

Facilitation and effective meetings

There's a huge difference between leading and facilitation and many times managers misappropriate those two skills in their job as a manager. That creates less than optimal outcome from the conducted events. Sometimes, this is the boring part of management because you have to support the logistics of the team and run meetings and events.

One of the key tools that a manager uses to effectively manage a team is meetings. This may sound trivial in a sense that anybody can run a meeting then how it's a tool for management. Here are few reasons why meeting is such an important tool:

- This is the most efficient way to disseminate information in a face-to-face manner to a group of people.
- Decision making can be done (with necessary legworks done ahead of that) in a meeting that is considered transparent and most impactful. Even in many cases, you can't make a decision without calling a formal meeting.
- Brainstorming, ideation, formal project management meetings, etc. are a few examples that only can be done in meeting settings.
- If you use Agile Scrum, then there are events that are done only in meeting settings, such as Daily Standup, Sprint Planning, Backlog Grooming, Sprint Review and Retro.

There are many more reasons but I am sure you already got the importance and benefit of meeting. As a manager you will sometimes conduct meetings and many times be part of meetings. So, knowing the mechanics of meetings would make a difference in your management outcome. Make sure you always plan for a GREAT meeting: Goal Oriented, Right people, Expectation clarified, Agenda in advance, and Time sensitivity.

Mechanics

- Unless there is a real urgent scenario, never schedule a team meeting without prior notice, better to give at least a day to let them prepare. Also, carefully choose the timing of the meeting. Suppose, if you want

a brainstorming meeting and you schedule it at 4:30 pm, the chance is that you will find them exhausted or lack the energy to engage with others. ⚠
- Think about the meeting logistics needed to run the meeting successfully: the board, marker, papers, projectors, screen, videos, audios, etc. The meeting rooms, if physically meeting, should be conducive to the purpose of the meeting.
- Create an agenda beforehand and send with the schedule. Never schedule a meeting with a blank agenda.
- In the meeting, go through the agenda items. Allow everyone to talk while you work as the time-keepers. As a facilitator, if you don't "time" discussions, the meeting time will be eaten up by not only unnecessary or conjectural topics but may also sabotage the agenda itself.
- Finally, ensure note taking either by yourself or by someone else. If you can't send a meaningful summary of the meeting of decisions made with appropriate action items, then it's like you've a wonderful 55 yard run and missed the touchdown in a foot game. You would be surprised that people create their own personalized meeting outcomes and carry that with them unless a written meeting outcome is distributed. Moreover, this also resolves any disagreement in the meeting outcome early enough.

Networking and building Relationships

Manager or not, you are sure to use these two skills in your day-to-day life. Let me first motivate you the value of these skills, both in Technical and People management perspectives.

Sometimes we disparagingly speak about "politics" at the workplace. We all hate it and for valid reasons. However, we sometimes don't understand that it's not the politics that ruined the workplace's sanity but it's the evil of human behavior injected into the "politics" that causes that corruption. Politics is nothing but working with fellow human beings to understand the power structure and use it for the benefit of people surrounding us. Albeit, we can't distinguish human behavior around us, that's why we blame "politics" altogether. Even though building networks and Relationships itself isn't politics, the outcome of that is of the same kind. Through this skill you understand the power structure of the organization. That's not necessarily finding powerful people but to know how an organization is structured and traverse through that structure to efficiently accomplish your managerial goals in an ethical manner.

As a technical manager, you are also responsible for the architecture and design of the software systems. These soft skills that are apparently have no technical significance but you would be surprised to know that your software architecture would be defined or at the very least, shaped by the people you know and the people you have access to. That aspect is nicely theorized by Conway's Law of Software Architecture. This has also been covered in the chapter under Technical Skills but it'll not be disservice if I repeat it here. Conway's law states: "Any organization that designs a system (defined broadly) will produce a design whose structure is a copy of the organization's communication structure." This indicates the strong bias that would influence the technical design based on whom you know and talk frequently. By being aware of this law, you would be more prepared when designing software systems[19].

Benefits

- The broader the network you build, the more effective and efficient your systems architecture would become. That's Conway's Law of Systems Architecture. Thanks to the higher access of systems and tools in your organization, your organization's software architect would be able to tap them to create the most effective systems architecture.
- You have to always look for talents inside and outside of your organization to build the best software development team. The larger network and stronger relationship with talented people will increase your chance of building a high performing team. I would also argue that without a strong network and relationship your ability to find talents would be very limited. Finding talents through traditional interviews is very expensive and error prone. Few hours of an interview can't be replaced by the long-lasting relationship of people.

Chapter 3: People Skills of a Manager

- This is true for every role in a software development career and very true for you as a manager - you would also be looking to get to the next step of your career ladder. The way you are always in hunt for talents, in the same way senior level managers are looking for talented managers like you. So, having effective networking and relationships would increase your chance to grow in your career.

Mechanics

These are like a laundry list of networking mechanics, so pick and choose that fits with your style.

- Start with your organization's provided networking opportunities. Check with your manager and Human Resource unit to find what are the professional networking groups or clubs that you can join. Examples of such networking groups could be: Professional development (e.g., Mentoring program), Management interest-based (e.g., PMP), Technology interest (e.g., AWS Architecture), Ethnic or Religious, Athletics, Volunteering, etc. Find your match based on your interest.
- Join workshops, seminars, roadshows, etc. that are occasionally organized in your organization or by your relevant professional domain.
- Join professional networking organizations such as Project Management Institute (PMI), CIO forums, IEEE, ACM, etc.
- If you have the opportunity to join workshops, conferences, etc. then those are fantastic opportunities to meet new people outside of your organization.
- Use professional social networking like LinkedIn. Create your profile, add people of interest into your network, write articles and share your area of interest that will attract people to your network.
- If such opportunity doesn't exist then your only option remains is to directly reach out within your peer organizations and beyond. Never shy away from calling or sending messages directly to anyone of your interest. Steve Jobs had mentioned his experience of calling Bill Hewlett, the Co-founder of Hewlett Packard (HP) asking for spare parts to build

his frequency-counter. He not only just got the spare parts but he also gave Steve Jobs a job in HP later on in the manufacturing line of building frequency-counter. So never underestimate starting your networking through a cold-call, if needed.
- One aspect of networking and building relationships that many professionals miss out is to appreciate that these are beyond transactional relationships. You don't build that to gain immediate benefit but you build that for the future. The less you use your network in a transactional manner, the better your chance to get help from your network and relationship.
- Finally, always keep contact with your network. That doesn't mean that you have to constantly talk to them but reach out to them periodically even if it's once in a quarter or may even be in a year, but do it.

Mentoring

Mentoring is showing others the journey of your (or someone in the similar role) own in an abstract way with real life examples so that the mentee can embark on that journey and create their own plan. Remember that you don't want to tell them what to do and what to become but you are only showing them the possibility in themselves and what they can choose to be. The mentee subsequently owns the direction taken. You, as a mentor, support them with their journey along the way.

The mentoring process can be summarized as-

- Create a trusted relationship between you and the mentee where the mentee can freely talk to you without feeling any fear of repercussion. That largely falls on you to build that image where your direct reports whose career depends on you yet they trust you. This is a tricky and delicate dance.
- Once the trust-based relationship is established, you understand the background, aspiration, strength and weakness of the mentee.
- Ask them to set their goal - the goal that has no boundary and limitation except their own will - a blue sky goal.

- Create a roadmap for the journey of the mentee - be sure to create the journey to the goal that they want to reach instead of you setting their goal.
- Be with them at every stage of their journey – be it in their success moment or at failure point. Provide the necessary support needed for your mentee to reach the goal of the mentorship.

Coaching

Coaching is similar to Mentoring but it's different in terms of ownership: you both jointly own the journey and you set a path for them to follow. Coaching is more for the members in your team who don't have the ability to create their own plan in career development. You may as well use coaching in other areas of management and leadership other than career development. As a coach you create a plan, motivate the employees, execute the plan and course correct if the plan doesn't go as expected.

You may only be familiar with coaching in the area of sports which is truly the originating place of this faculty. However, as a manager and leader of your team your role isn't very different from that of a football or soccer coach performing in their day-to-day job. You may ignore this area and may feel just fine managing people but if you can acquire some traits of a coach, you would be able to create your brand image in the organization and be able to retain and attract talents to your team. Here's an outline on how you can coach your direct report:

- Assess their current strengths, weaknesses and potential growth areas.
- Come up with the career SMART goals: short term (3 - 6 months), medium term (6 - 12 months) and long term (1 - 3 years). The SMART goals should be: Specific, Measurable, Achievable, Relevant and Time bound. Example of a SMART goal is John F Kennedy's famous speech: that the country "should commit itself to achieving the goal, before this decade is out, of landing a man on the Moon and returning him safely to the Earth."

- Create a set of action plans to achieve the goals. Identify the resources needed to reach the goals and the gap in their skills. Specify the reward if they achieve the goals.
- Schedule periodic check-in meetings to review the progress and provide your feedback.
- If necessary, course-correct their execution or change the goals if the need of the person or your organization changes.
- Make sure the initially set rewards are awarded.

Managing Working Remote

After COVID19 pandemic, the world has changed and working remotely is not an exception anymore but part of work-norm. There are two aspects of working remotely: individual contributor's remote working and a manager's managing in a remote setting. As this book is a guide for the manager, I am only covering how you would manage your remote work.

First, create a remote working etiquette. Like, when to use video and when not to, how to inform others in the team about your unavailability, etc.

- Use of written communications becomes paramount in the remote working setting.
- Create a "Water Cooler Moment" while all are working remotely. Water cooler conversations are one of the most critical social interactions to build networks, foster creativity, validate your ideas and many more positive effects.
- Meeting and then breakout sessions for developers to foster networking. Use of a whiteboard (or collaboration document) are key tools for a successful remote meeting.
  - Small initiatives with random people as a group/team
  - Create club/interest group
  - Mentorship program
- You can also create a remote working policy, to create the effectiveness among the team members. Set norms for team interaction while remote.
  - Specific norms and rules to be available online. E.g., use of messenger's status (available, away, out of office, work-location, etc.)

- o To have in-person experience, use Camera during a meeting.
- o For one-on-one calls, unless there's constraint, turn on both of your cameras.
- o For meetings, unless the expectation is set by the meeting moderator, the camera should be turned on.
- o Use visual tools to share ideas. Use of online collaboration sites and tools (touch pad) is preferrable.
- Few other examples of foster collaborative work environment are:
  - o Small initiatives with random people as a group/team
  - o Create club/interest group
  - o Mentorship program
- Location still matters even if you're working remote:
  - o In a remote work setting, they can work from anywhere as it's remote, however, the time zone and other geographic factors may impact your team members ability to work effectively. So, make sure that they are aware of the policy on reviewing with you first before deciding to move to some other geographical time zone.
  - o There can't be one fit for all as the level of expertise, manageability, customer's expectation, data security or access policy, etc. impact where remote working can be done from. So be open to individualized need to decide your team's request to choose on working remote locations.

PART III

Process aspects of ***Management***

Project and Organization

Gone are those days where software companies or even any IT companies are structured in only one organizational form: either Functional or Project organization. Most if not all software companies use the Matrix form of those two structures. Even if your organization isn't using Matrix structure, be sure that the software development would utilize the Matrix organization.

Functional organization takes care of the functional needs such as career development, allocation of engineers into the appropriate projects, cross train skill and most optimal allocation of skills across projects. This structure is usually technology focused such as Software Engineer (Frontend, Backend, Full Stack), Database Developer, SQA, DevOps, Architecture, etc. This can be done in an outcome focused area such as Product Development, Consultant Services, R&D, Architecture, Production Support, Release Management, etc. A manager in the functional organization mostly plays the role of a career development manager. The actual software development goes mostly to the Development Manager, Development Lead or a Technical Project Manager.

Project organization is responsible for the delivery of the project goal within the structure of the project. The functional organization provides the human resources and project organization is responsible to run through the lifecycle of the project. Software Developers mostly have a matrix reporting to the Functional Managers and Project Managers. However, many times, functional managers wear the hat of a development manager or technical project manager in a project organization. That all depends on the scope, size and on company work culture.

Below is a sample of the Matrix Organization where an individual reports to their functional division and being a part of a project, reports to a Project Manager.

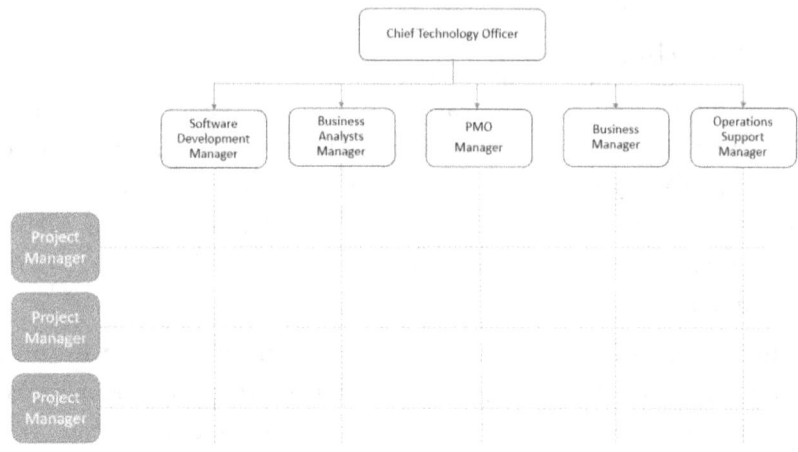

Figure - 4: Sample Matrix organization template[3]

Regardless of where you are placed in the organization structure, as a Software Development Manager, the more you're skilled in software development processes the better are your chances to be successful. In the next few chapters, you will get to know the key process management skills that includes, Software Project Management, Software Development Methodologies (including Scrum), Software Requirement Management, Cost Estimation, and Software Quality Management.

CHAPTER IV

Chapter 4: Software Project Management

PMI defines project management as "Project management is the use of specific knowledge, skills, tools and techniques to deliver something of value to people. The development of software for an improved business process, the construction of a building, the relief effort after a natural disaster, the expansion of sales into a new geographic market—these are all examples of projects."

Project is defined as "...temporary efforts to create value through unique products, services, and processes."[4]

The most important characteristics of a project is the temporal nature of it i.e., a certain beginning and a predetermined end time with an agreed upon goal to achieve. That sets a project from all other operational types of work. Also, this very nature of the "temporal" nature of the project makes it so attractive that almost all software is now developed as Projects. So, even though you as a Software Development Manager isn't a Project Manager, I would strongly recommend you to change your mindset if you think you won't need to understand project management as part of a software development management role. Sooner you accept it better for you to be more impactful in your role.

Project Management is relatively a new management technique compared to the existence of traditional management practice that mostly covers the operational aspects of management. The rise of projects made the Project Manager a new thriving role for the last few decades. Software Development, coincidentally, became a thriving industry for the last few decades. If not all, the majority of the software development follows the project management approach. I am intentionally isolating the software support work from the software development because you don't need a software development manager to support a software that is in operation. Any qualified traditional manager can effectively manage that kind of work. The other reason why software development better suits the project management rather than traditional management i.e., operation management: every software development endeavor is a creative work and building the software or even enhancing the software falls cleanly on

Chapter 4: Software Project Management

the definition of the Project which is - creating something new with a definite beginning and end.

Clarifying a bigger question: do you need to be PMP certified or follow the PMI defined project management practice in your role? If you already have one, good for you. If you don't have one, I would argue that most of the time you won't need most of those skills unless you are moving to a full time Project Manager role. Also, there are reason, why I wouldn't recommend you to learn the PMP processes from PMI at this point of your journey for the below reasons:

- PMI has a very rigid project management structure with 47 project management processes within 5 Project Management Process Groups and 10 Knowledge Areas. Many times, those are not always applicable in software development in comparison to other domains. Unless you're in a government project where PMP is a prerequisite, then that's a different discussion.
- Most of the time, you will have someone who would play the PM role so you will need to collaborate with them instead of running them. So, if you have overview knowledge of project management to collaborate with PMs that should be good enough.
- Software development, most of the time, is a people driven technical endeavor with heavy focus on people management and technical architecture & design. So, many times, Project Management is made lightweight for the heavy dependency of the human side. As for instance, a construction project to build a bridge or a rocket ship. The procurement management is one of the most complex parts of the project unlike a regular software development project.
- Finally, if you're given a task to both manage the software developers and run a project like a PM, I am pretty sure that your project isn't that complex or large that would demand you to run the project with the full breadth and depth of PMI's Project Management processes. Nonetheless, if you are required in depth knowledge of a PMP, you can take a break from this book, prepare for the PMP and get back to this book once you're certified.

Before I move on to the necessary details of Software Project Management, let me provide a summary structure of the PMI project Management framework as defined in the Project Management Book of Knowledge (PMBOK)[20] with a short description.

Project Management Processes are grouped into 5 Process Groups:

Initiating Process Group: "consists of those processes performed to define a new project or a new phase of an existing project by obtaining authorization. Within the Initiating processes, the initial scope is defined and initial financial resources are committed. Internal and external stakeholders who will interact and influence the overall outcome of the project are identified." to start the project or phase.

Planning Process Group: "consists of those processes performed to establish the total scope of the effort, define and refine the objectives, and develop the course of action required to attain those objectives. The Planning processes develop the project management plan and the project documents that will be used to carry out the project."

Executing Process Group: "consists of those processes performed to complete the work defined in the project management plan to satisfy the project specifications. This Process Group involves coordinating people and resources, managing stakeholder expectations, as well as integrating and performing the activities of the project in accordance with the project management plan."

Monitoring & controlling Process Group: "consists of those processes required to track, review and orchestrate the progress and performance of the project; identify any areas in which changes to the plan are required; and initiate the corresponding changes."

Project Closing Process Group: "consists of those processes performed to conclude all activities across all Project Management Processes Groups to formally complete the project, phase, or contractual obligations. This Process Group, when completed, verifies that the defined processes are completed within all the Process Groups to close the project or a project

Chapter 4: Software Project Management

phase, as appropriate, and formally establishes that the project or project phase is complete."

Under those process groups, the below knowledge areas are covered:

- Project Integration Management
- Project Scope Management
- Project Time Management
- Project Cost Management
- Project Quality Management
- Project Human Resources Management
- Project Communication Management
- Project Risk Management
- Project Procurement Management
- Project Stakeholder Management

Instead of going over the above 10 Knowledge Areas, I will go by the Process Groups that are relevant for a software project.

Why is Project Management absolutely critical to be a Development Manager?

You may or may not do any of the project management processes as a Software Development Manager and especially if there's a dedicated Project Manager engaged in your project. However, you should know it to be able to manage your development resources and people effectively and partnership with the PM.

Project Management framework for Software

Project oriented processes cover the initiation of a project through the closure of the project. The actual development of the software falls under the Project Execution. So, if you're asked to manage the project then use the below management practices. However, if you're given a PM to manage the project or you are collaborating with a PM as part of your role, make sure that at the very least, these project management practices take place. These will not only increase the chance of the project's success but also will make your life much easier as you will have a structured process that you can predict ahead of time thus planning better for your development team(s).

Chapter 4: Software Project Management

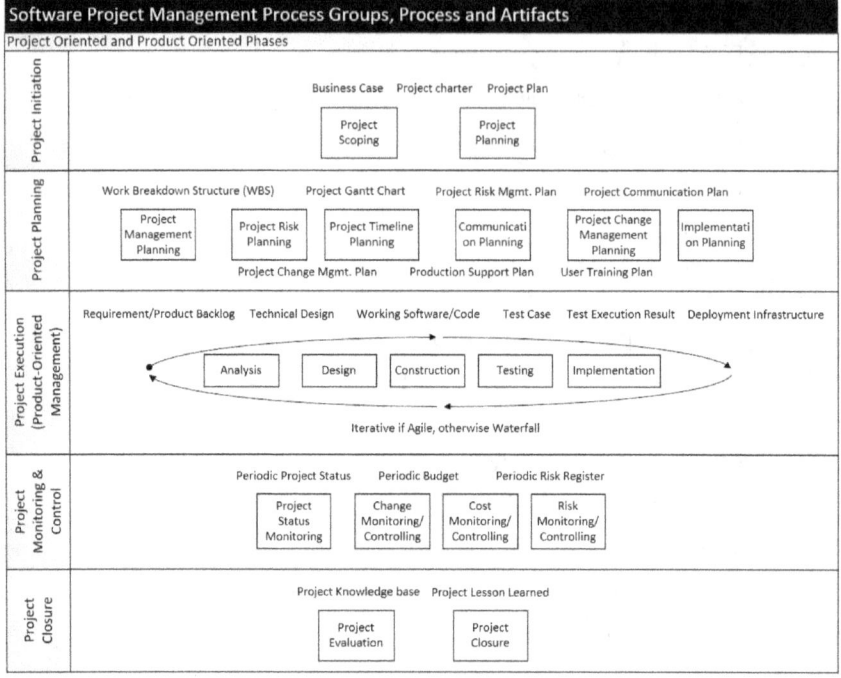

Figure-5: Overview of Software Project Management

Project oriented management

The Project-oriented aspect covers all the processes and stages to run a project that's usually indifferent from what software is being built. As a matter of fact, the Project-oriented management processes are in many cases agnostic whether it's a software project or any other project. This also provides a structure surrounding the product development.

Project Initiation

The project initiation is the formal beginning of the project life cycle. At the time of project initiation phase, the project's charter is created that defines the objective of the project, the budget, stakeholders (people and roles who are positively or negatively impacted due to this project), and official approval to kick off the project.

Best practices:

- Regardless of being asked or not, create a Project Charter that formally authorizes a project to kick off. It doesn't matter if you write it using a nice formatted template or just sending an email to your superior or customer, nonetheless, do it meticulously. You, and every one of you in the project will inevitably forget why the project was needed (the original business value) in the first place, how much money was agreed to spend and for how long, and what the original project's expected outcome was. If you need to manage the budget as part of this, make sure you have a section in the charter write up.
- Define the scope of Project. To make it very explicit: define the Scope of Project's deliverable, not the Software Product itself. You're going to build the product's scope as part of the Product Oriented Management process group. Some example deliverables are: Business Case, Project Charter and Project Plans, Prototype of User Interface (wireframe), Technical Design document, Testing Strategy and Test plan, Training Plan and materials, etc.
- Define the Stakeholders: who is providing you the money, who is going to use your software and who will be approving the software before commissioning. Most of the stakeholders would be either contributing to the success of the project or may remain as bystanders. However, there might even be a few stakeholders who actively or passively want to see your project not succeeded. You have to be aware and manage both types of stakeholders.

Project Planning

There are various levels of planning involved in a project. Depending on the scope and size of the project, you may decide to do certain planning and skip others. But at least knowing the planning processes would help you to be aware of it.

Project Management Plan states how the work will be performed. The plan consists of Project Timeline Plan, Work Breakdown Structure, Project Risk Management plan, Project Communication Plan, etc.

Work Breakdown Structure (WBS) is a traditional way to define the Project Scope and break down the planned work into smaller manageable tasks. However, if you use Agile methodology, the WBS would contain a Product Backlog (PB) for the software product requirement. The most critical part of planning the WBS and PB is to estimate the work. The detailed technique of Cost Estimation is covered in the *Requirement Management and Cost Estimation* chapter. Once you've done the estimation, you can create the project timeline.

Project Timeline Plan is the most sought-after document by customer which is often given in the form of the famous artifact: Gantt chart. It creates a timeline view of the detailed work with people and resources assigned to each task. The Milestones are clearly defined. A Critical Path Analysis should be done to identify the tasks and resources that fall on a critical path. Missing any of those tasks or resources would risk the project' time commitment.

Project Risk Management Plan covers how the project risks would be identified, tracked and then mitigated throughout the life of a project. Risk Register contains the risks identified to track transparently by assigning each risk a Risk Owner who would be responsible to take the risk to a closed state. An important part of Risk management is the strategy to mitigate the identified risks. Not all risks need to be addressed in the same manner, some of those can be avoided, some of those can be transferred to a third party (e.g., insurance plan). For the risks that can't be avoided or transferred, as a last resort, handle those head on.

Project Change Management Plan may sound very bureaucratic and yes, they become bureaucratic at times, however, even if you want to keep it sweet and simple, document the plan and circulate it to the project team. It's important to know how the project changes would be analyzed, prioritized and resolved. Lack of a bare minimum change management plan, a project may suffer scope creep or unhappy customers even after everything is delivered by the project team.

Project Communication Plan is often ignored in many projects. However, an effective communication plan and its timely execution may make the difference between a successful project and a failed project. This plan is often taken as a pulse check of a solid project management plan. The last thing the stakeholders want to see from you as a manager is a long awkward silence on the project's status. Cover, at the very least, below points in the communication plan:

- What artifact would be used to share the status of the project and in what frequency?
- How the project risks would be communicated?
- How to reach out to the project team i.e., the communication medium (phone, email, meeting, project website, wiki, etc.)?
- What's the escalation mechanism and escalation contacts?

Project Execution

Project's execution has two flavors: the Project-oriented management and the Product-oriented management i.e., the SDLC. The Product's SDLC is covered in the later section hence only the Project-oriented management part is explained here. The Project and Product executions are intertwined so you can't get one successful without doing both the executions right.

For Execution, the first thing you do is to kick off a Software Development Team. This is different from the Project team. The development team would be structured according to your SDLC - if you use Scrum, then follow the Scrum team structure. However, if you do not use Scrum, then create a development team, the cadence, and necessary team documentation to kick off the actual building of the software.

Note: the *chapter: Software Development Manager* has covered how to build a team, the phases of team building and how to make the team efficient. So, refer to that in the project execution.

Project Monitoring & Controlling

Project needs to be monitored at all times and courses corrected as and when needed. It's easy to say but how do you monitor projects? And what do you monitor? Answering the last question first: you monitor everything: project risks, project scope and its changes, project cost, project quality, and above all, the health of the project team.

There are many ways to implement project monitoring and control and below are some of the best practices that you can easily add to your management toolbox:

- Meet with the project team periodically: with the team in a group setting and with every project member or at least with the key individuals in one-on-one setting. These are the tools that would give you the pulse of a project more than it gives through the project status report or a PowerPoint slide. Watch for any deteriorating aspect in team motivation, frustration, and dedication. Among other factors, those are the barometer of the project team's health check.
- Periodically review the project risk register and communicate with the project team if a new risk is being materialized.
- Monitor the project cost, if you have access to it. If you don't have access to the whole budget, at the very least make sure to get the software development budget that you're more dependable to it. Monitor how much is spent against the budget. This is the bottom-line that is sometimes amendable but most of the time the more efficient you are to manage the project bottom-line, the better goodwill you will have with your stakeholders and project sponsors.
- It's important to have a predictable routine for everything that you are to monitor - be it weekly, bi-weekly or monthly - depending on the size and duration of the project. Better to do it in a group setting but if you don't or can't do it, at least do it regularly with key individuals and plan your actions accordingly.
- Finally, the most important thing any manager and leader needs to excel is to predict the upcoming events. The sooner you can "weather forecast" your project, the better your reaction time would be. You have to understand both the micro and macro factors of projects. Micro project-factors are those that you can get from the project itself i.e., cost, risks, scope, change, stakeholders, etc. However, the macro project-factors are the company's vision, long term goal, potential of the project and company market segment, other competing projects, the macroeconomic factors of the country, and ultimately the world

geopolitical circumstances. If that sounds too much, yes, it's too much. You don't have to put all the macro project-factors in your head to be able to manage your project; however, if you can use some of them, then you would be ahead of the curve in the game.

Project Closure

Project closure consists of two activities: Project Closing with due diligence and conduct Lessons Learned from which the next projects can be benefited.

Depending on the nature of the project, a Project Closing can be tedious or simple. If there's any regulatory requirement, make sure you check all the boxes. Close any vendor or third-party agreements. The last but most important step is to dismantle the project team. The ramping down may have started early and gradually closed the team. As a Software Development Manager, your most important responsibility is to find new projects or work for the Developers in your organization. That shouldn't wait for this moment but if the developers are not assigned to other projects, then this should be the essential part of the project closure action items.

Project Evaluation is the very last step in the life of a project. There are many things that can be done and needs to be done but at the minimum do the Lessons Learned i.e., Retrospective. You may have done this event as part of SDLC (in Scrum it is called as Sprint Retro) however at this stage you do it at project-level and ask the similar questions: what went well, what didn't go well and what could've been done differently. Document the outcome of the lesson learned discussion along with all other project documents in your company Project Knowledgebase, if available, or at any company's common shared storage location. Future project managers and Development Managers would thank you and be obliged to you for this information.

Product oriented management

As part of Product oriented management, the Systems Development Life Cycle (SDLC) is defined, planned, executed and managed. Always remember: if you use Agile, it's imperative but it's important to remember that: regardless of the SDLC you use, you must use automation (CI/CD) in the implementation.

Analysis

As part of Analysis, you define the scope of the software product: the Functional Requirements or Features of the product, Non-functional Requirements (or often called as Quality Attributes in Software Architectural terminology) like Performance expectation, Security, User Experience (UX) expectations, Maintainability, Testability, etc.

Design

If you use Agile, then use the Agile architecture and design described in the *Software Development Methodologies* and *Software Design Review* chapters. In the case of Agile SDLC, you will create a very high-level design at this stage and continue the cycle of *Analysis - Design - Construction - Testing - Implementation* throughout the execution phase. Making sure to have an effective Technical Design Review process to make sure the architecture of the software is kept within the range of the quality threshold.

Construction

At this stage, the making of the working software is done. Again, for Agile development methods (e.g., Scrum), this is done in the cycle of *Analysis - Design - Construction - Testing - Implementation*. Making sure to use Code Quality standards measurements are taken through coding review (e.g., Lead review, Peer review, etc.).

Testing

Testing is the method for Project Quality management in the software project. Chapter *Software Quality Management* has detailed out how to ensure the software quality, use that during this stage. As mentioned earlier, if your project follows Agile SDLC, this would follow the cycle of *Analysis - Design - Construction - Testing - Implementation.*

Implementation

The final stage of the execution phase is implementing the software to the production environment. Depending on your SDLC (e.g., if it's Agile), then you may do more frequent deployment than just one big bang deployment. However, regardless of how many times you do the deployment, you should have an implementation plan prepared and executed at this stage. Few things to remember at this stage:

- Have a concrete production support plan and procedure in place before rolling out the software.
- Production systems monitoring should be planned ahead. Use automation in monitoring.

Project Management is like an ocean of knowledge so, if you find it interesting and want to become expert in project management, feel free to deep dive more by taking courses or reading books or even go for PMP certification. However, this chapter tries to give you a high level of project management in the context of software development to prepare you for a successful role as Software Development Manager.

Chapter 5: Software Development Methodologies

Chapter 5: Software Development Methodologies

If you came from a developer's background then you may have already used one or more of the Systems Development Life Cycle (SDLC) methodologies. You may even be an expert of one SDLC methodology that you have used for a long time. However, as a manager, now you not only have to understand those methodologies but also understand the pros-and-cons of the available methodologies. Because you have to now compare the situations and decide which SDLC methodology would be a good fit for your project and team. A small software project that is to be done by a developer is completely different from working in a team environment where various roles are in play by different members of the team for a quite long period. Imposing a methodology for that small project would be a huge overhead whereas ignoring the need for a development process in a long running (for months or even years) project with a team would be a fallacy. There are various software development methodologies that one can utilize. Some of the well-known and efficient methodologies are Scrum, Extreme Programming, Rational Unified Process, etc. Due to the sheer popularity of Agile methodology, we can divide all these into two broad categories: Agile (e.g., Scrum, Kanban, XP, TDD, etc.) and non-Agile (e.g., RUP) methodologies.

There exist various types of SDLC that fits for various development situations:

- Waterfall development methodology
- Iterative process
- Agile methodology
- Hybrid of Waterfall and Agile

Even though you may have heard that Waterfall is a dead SDLC, I argue that there are still projects out there, albeit smaller in number, that fit better in Waterfall than Agile. Nonetheless, the most important reason to learn the Waterfall is to broaden your knowledge even if you are not in need of such SDLC and thus prepare you for the more practical methodology which is *the Hybrid SDLC*.

Waterfall development methodology

This is the more traditional method of SDLC until the rise of Agile methodology in the 1990s. The Waterfall method is very simple to grasp and, like its name, flows sequentially from requirement gathering to implementation without repeating it. This simple depiction of the stages of the waterfall method shows it all.

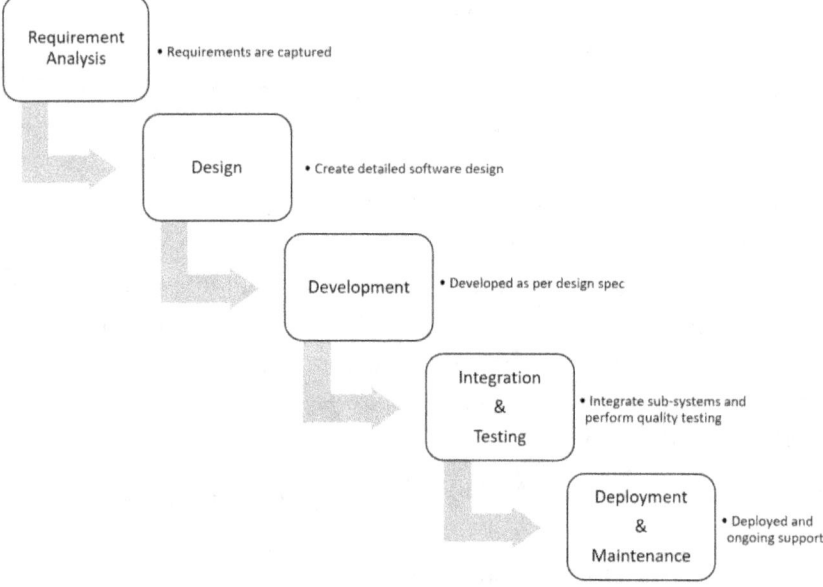

Figure-6: Depiction of Waterfall method[5]

At the Requirement Gathering stage, a group of Analysts or Software Developers collect the entire project requirement and capture that in a formal document like Business Requirement Definition (BRD), or Use Case if the development is primarily done using Object Oriented Principles. The expectation is that all the nitty-gritty details are captured in that requirement artifact which the customers or the end-users provide a sign-off and off you go to start the Architecture and Design of the software. That sounds so logical that nobody questioned for quite a long time whether it is realistic to capture every detail at the beginning without experiencing a tangible working software to test out the requirement

Chapter 5: Software Development Methodologies

"hypothesis". Yes, I am calling the requirement as "a hypothesis" because until the software is built, the customer is hypothesizing that those requirements would meet the need of the business. Thus, building the software and working as expected is the "proof" of that hypothesis.

Requirement Gathering

In the Waterfall method, the first stage is gathering requirements for the entire software product. The requirements are then reviewed and signed-off by the customer. Once the requirement is finalized that becomes a contract and nothing can be changed without a strict change management process. The software development then moves into the Design phase.

Design

In this phase, the software is designed to the "Nth" degree. Every system's detail, integration interface, Class and Method signature, Package diagram, deployment diagram, etc. everything is designed at a very detailed level. This design is also approved by the customer before the implementation starts. Once the Software design is approved, that can't be changed without the same strict change management process.

Implementation & Development

Coding starts at this stage and continues by the software development team until they meet all the customer's approved requirements. Usually, customers never see the software till the completion of development. Once the development is complete then individual components or subsystems are tested in isolation.

Integration & Test

The integration with components and subsystems is done afterwards and goes through integration testing. This is a major milestone and nerve-wrecking because if a major flaw is identified at this stage, that may take the project back to square one.

Deployment

Customer's approval allows the software product to go into the final state of implementation and deploy to the Production environment. By contract, the entire software goes live in one shot which is known as the "Big Bang" approach.

Operations and Maintenance

Post-production operation support is provided to the customer and ongoing maintenance continues.

Advantages of Waterfall method:

Even the waterfall method has some advantages if it's used for the right kind of project, such as, repeat implementation of the same solution, like ERP, CRM, etc. In those cases, it's important to make sure that the domain and solution is very close to the previous implementation. If there are limited surprises expected in the requirement and implementation, the waterfall method provides predictability to the project i.e., time, resources and budget.

Disadvantages of Waterfall method:

Waterfall is one of the culprits of most software project's failures. The disadvantages are so long that it would become a book of itself. To provide a few prominent disadvantages:

- It's very costly to capture the requirement in such great detail at the beginning of the project that may go for years. Sometimes requirements get changed not because the requirements itself has changed but the business or customer's needs have changed by that time. We live in a constantly changing world where we have less control in our business than we think we do. COVID19 was a mega example where the entire economy had to react to the pandemic. Even if you don't have that drastic change in business, there are constant changes in economy, geopolitics, customer, competition, etc. that will inevitably lead to requirement changes.
- The integration is the nerve-wrecking event in the waterfall method. It's like Aircraft or Rocketship development where thousands of parts need to fit perfectly to work whereas software is nothing like Aircraft or Rocketship development. The very nature of software development creates integration risk if they aren't done frequently.

Chapter 5: Software Development Methodologies

- Big-bang deployment approach has a major drawback. Apart from not being able to get customers feedback, this approach proves detrimental to the inability to predict the load in the systems. Obama care's Health Insurance Exchange was one such example when it went live and didn't work for weeks due to unanticipated customer's load and integration bottleneck caused by the legacy systems inability to scale.
- Waterfall method was copied from large scale project implementation in other domains like Civil engineering, Mechanical Engineering, Electrical Engineering, Urban Development, etc. It took time to recognize that Software engineering is nothing like Civil/Mechanical/Electrical engineering. Many things can be said but the top most reason is: as software can be changed very easily in a matter of one line code change or configuration in the database even after it goes to production, which is also the selling point of software, so software changes tremendously throughout the lifecycle of the software development unlike a bridge, an aircraft, a factory, or a road network.

Iterative Development Process

Waterfall clearly showed its deficiencies and consistently failing large projects, the introduction of Iterative SDLC became inevitable. Rational Unified Process (RUP)[6] was the most successful in the beginning of this millennium. This method creates a mini-waterfall within an iteration and reduces the chances of failing big. The phases were usually:

Inception

"In this phase the business case which includes business context, success factors (expected revenue, market recognition, etc.), and a financial forecast is established." [6]

Elaboration

"The primary objective is to mitigate the key risk items identified by analysis up to the end of this phase. The elaboration phase is where the project starts to take shape. In this phase the problem domain analysis is made and the architecture of the project gets its basic form." [6]

Construction

"The primary objective is to build the software system. In this phase, the main focus is on the development of components and other features of the system. This is the phase when the bulk of the coding takes place. In larger projects, several construction iterations may be developed in an effort to divide the use cases into manageable segments to produce demonstrable prototypes." [6]

Transition i.e., Implementation

In this phase, the software is delivered to the customer, the post production support is provided and ongoing maintenance continues.

The entire project life cycle is broken into a number of Phases, Iterations and Milestones and continue until the end of the project delivery. Here's the famous image depicting the RUP[7]:

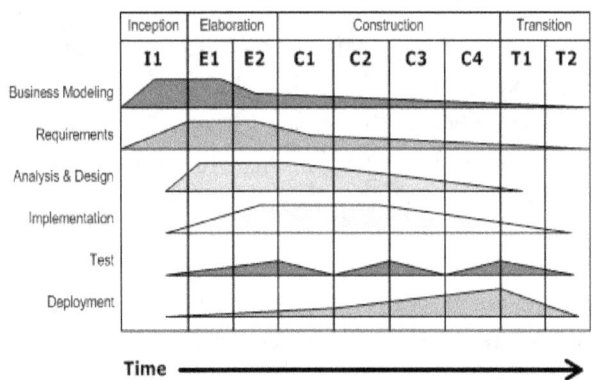

Figure-7: Rational Unified Process

RUP was a licensed process that Rational (bought by IBM afterwards) brought a suite of tools to implement it. It was targeted for large enterprise software projects and rather bulky in nature. This is now considered a dead process. However, if you're interested in reviving this process in your project, read this whitepaper: Rational Unified Process – An Introduction[8].

Agile

Agile has many implementations which you can learn but the most popular and widespread Agile framework is Scrum. Other Agile methodologies are: XP, TDD, Pair Programming, etc. However, only Scrum provides the management aspects of the SDLC that covers a complete delivery of a software implementation project. The details of Scrum are covered later in the book (chapter x: Software Development Methodology and chapter x: Deep Dive to Agile Scrum). Read those two chapters to get the mechanics on how Agile and Scrum methodology actually work. For now, let's see few of the assumptions that Scrum makes:

- The enterprise organization and its processes, such as project initiation, budgeting, risk management, stakeholder management and communication, etc. are taken care of by outside of the Scrum SDLC.
- The Team members i.e., Developers are superstars. They can analyze the requirement, talk to the customers to gather requirements, they can architect, they can test, they can deploy. So, the Developers are multi-talented and change the hats as and when needed.
- Without those above assumptions in place, an ideal Scrum team can't function. You will see later in this chapter why Hybrid methodology is becoming popular because of these two assumptions which often are not practical.

Agile Software Development

Agile software development can and should be summarized through the Agile Manifesto, adopted in 2001,

"We are uncovering better ways of developing software by doing it and helping others do it.

Chapter 5: Software Development Methodologies

> *Through this work we have come to value:*
> *Individuals and interactions over processes and tools*
> *Working software over comprehensive documentation*
> *Customer collaboration over contract negotiation*
> *Responding to change over following a plan*
> *That is, while there is value in the items on*
> *the right, we value the items on the left more."*
>
> Source: *http://agilemanifesto.org/*

No one can describe Agile better or in a more concise way than the above definition, however, if you need a further shortened version, here's my attempt to define Agile: Collaboratively working with users to create value through the continuous delivery of working software.

Myth and Truth about Agile

The term "Agile" has now become closer to a fad than true appreciation. You will see people brag about how "agile" they are in their software development organization. Not only that, but I have also seen people use the term "Agile" for activities such as project planning where no software development is involved at all. But who would counter them? You would be lectured by seasoned consultants by deconstructing word by word and how their method of creating a plan is a truly agile process. On the other hand, a person who claims to love Agile and lives in Agile will tell you how Agile development is much more superior to the "waterfall method". By the way, who will tell them that between the Stone Age and industrial age, there was Iron Age and don't compare the industrial age with the Stone Age by skipping the Iron Age civilization? With all those, I felt obligated to explain the "Truth" of Agile software development methodology. Let's begin with a simple fact.

Agile is for Software Development

Believe it or not, Agile is and came for software development. People may tell you otherwise by showing the linguistic deconstruction of noun vs.

Chapter 5: Software Development Methodologies

adjective and prove to you that Agile can be used for your apple picking job as well. For the record: I had once done an "Agile snow cleaning" in the winter - just to have fun as I was tired of snow cleaning due to a repeated blizzard that threw a couple of feet of snow. It was just for pure fun; no academic purpose was involved in that. But if anyone claims that Agile can be implemented anywhere, then I would argue that you can develop software using "Taekwondo" principles as well. Spinning can be endless.

Agile is not the successor of Waterfall methodology

As I had touched upon at the beginning, before Agile, Iterative methods were very successful and effective. If you ask me what method I would prefer: Agile Scrum or Iterative Rational Unified Process? I would tell you, pick any but be consistent

Agile is not a silver bullet

Businesses sometimes think that Agile is a silver bullet and solves every problem the business is facing today. Agile is rather a software development methodology that comes into existence to reduce the risk of software development and maximize the business value of software but it is not a panacea. Agile is not free of cost though. The cost includes the risk of losing a big picture of the solution, quicksand for architectural soundness, overemphasizing on working software over long-term stability, fading documentation, etc. Also, Agile demands certain creeds without that it is hard, if not impossible, to be successful. Though not all the risks are due to the Agile practice but sometimes because people use Agile as the scapegoat.

Agile needs business people to be involved...fully involved

When a business wants the IT to be Agile, they often don't realize that the Agile is not a methodology that IT will practice on their own and the business will continue their existing operational model. Agile needs business to change or adapt to the Agile development model. Business flocks into Agile to get the fruit of transparency on how it is being cooked in the kitchen but to reap that fruit of Agile, business needs to play their part. It takes two to tango!

Scrum is not synonymous to Agile

Scrum is widely popular in the industry over other Agile implementations such as Test-Driven Development (TDD), Extreme Programming (XP), etc. So, people who jumped late on the Agile bandwagon sometimes confused Scrum as the Agile process. Scrum is just one implementation of Agile that has given a framework to manage the Agile software development project very effectively. As Scrum has taken Agile close to the business people (because the other Agile implementations are too technical for non-technical business people to grasp), they have taken the familiarization with Agile through the Scrum framework.

Agile is a philosophy and demands a cultural change

The Agile Manifesto talks about the philosophy and principles behind the Agile Software Development methodology. Agile doesn't dictate one on how to achieve those principles but this can be said with a level of certainty that without changing the culture in software development, it is impossible to achieve those principles. I have seen instances where business sprinkles the principles of Agile software development on the engineering team without emphasizing the underlying cultural change and then blames Agile for their failure.

How to reap the best out of Agile

As we have debunked the myth of the Agile methodology, let's look into how we can get the best out of an Agile team. There are volumes of books, training, and certifications that are available on building and running Agile teams but here is a shortlist of best practices (or you may call them as principles if you will) to build a successful Agile team that produces the most value to its cost.

A quick disclaimer: for simplicity, this article is focused primarily on SCRUM Agile development methodology as the term "Agile" is more familiar than "SCRUM". So, one can use the word "SCRUM" and "Agile" interchangeably while reading this chapter

Chapter 5: Software Development Methodologies

Hire Team members who believe in Agile

Eric Schmidt, the former CEO of Google, has said in his book, "How Google Works" that Google doesn't transform a person into problem-solving ninja but the company attracts those ninjas and they build the great products at Google. So, if you want to get your Agile team to excel, hire the "smart creative" people who believe in Agile. Agile is a cultural mindset, not just a mere methodology that can be memorized. You can't turn or train people to become Agile unless they have that "Agile" gene deep into them. But you can tune them in Agile if that is what they believe in.

Now, let's talk in a practical term. Neither companies are Google nor would you have the freedom to pick your team at all the time. So, at the bare minimum, when you don't have that liberty to build from scratch, before putting them into a team for Agile, train them in Agile. Seriously! Train them in Agile!

Get business buy-in... This is the master key to success in Agile

In this chapter, I have explained the importance of having the business people fully engaged in the Agile process. Without the full participation of business, there's almost no chance of running the show in Agile. There are occasions where the Software Development teams claim that they are Agile without the business participating in it which is kind of an oxymoron and hard to believe.

So, if you cannot secure the buy-in of business into your Agile process, it is better to use other non-Agile methodologies, such as Rational Unified Process (RUP) or any other iterative method, except Waterfall. Believe it or not, those non-Agile methodologies work just fine when practiced consistently.

Avoid the quicksand of Architectural and Design soundness

Let's not use Agile as an excuse for a poor Architecture or a closed design. Yes, Agile doesn't let the team spend a lot of time to focus on a robust architecture and comprehensive software design rather emphasize on working software. It asks for minimal upfront design and continues to design throughout the product development life cycle. The crux of the game is "refactoring". The refactoring has to be done both at the code and design level. This means continuous rework and occasional throwaway code. If you are not ready to accept that notion of refactoring, maybe Agile isn't fit for your project.

There's a catch in that minimal upfront design though, which we forget often. The notion of "minimal upfront design" in Agile requires that the developers are skilled in design & architecture. Moreover, those Designers or Architects would be doing coding in the team. Your organization needs to be ready to invest in those people.

Still, you do Release Planning

Even though Project Management principles are in direct conflict with Agile principles, there's a fair amount of planning involved in Agile projects. What you have in traditional project management as Work Breakdown Structure, in an Agile project you would have Product Backlog with User Stories. Through Affinity Sizing the product backlog would give a sense of project duration which would be broken down into Releases based on business priority, value, and dependencies to get Agile Project Scheduling.

Some Agile practitioners feel very uncomfortable with this planning aspect of Agile that's based on affinity sizing. Affinity sizing is done at a high level of understanding with minimal detail. This lack of comfort is not the fault of those people but the fault lies in not utilizing the affinity sizing with the right intention. The affinity sizing can no way be used as the basis for commitment but the user stories have to go through multiple passes of refinement and resizing over the time to come to the level of confidence to make project commitments. The Cone of uncertainty in software estimation has to be kept in consideration when making commitments because "you can't beat the Cone of uncertainty but you just can be luckier"

Do the right Sprint planning, if you're using Scrum

Chapter 5: Software Development Methodologies

Task, Task, and Task....this is crucial that team members create the tasks for each user story! One of the objectives of the Sprint planning is to create tasks for the user stories. The purpose of keeping the Sprint shorter is to ensure that the developers can plan in detail and the manifestation of successful planning is "a lot of tasks". Human brains are not good at keeping every detail for the next few months and that's why the Sprints are recommended to keep between two to four weeks. This is a very crucial tool for a successful Sprint.

Yes, the first objective is to create the Sprint Backlog (scope) for the upcoming Sprint but the more important objective is to go into the next level to each of the stories and break them into tasks (tasks should be no more than that a day, and smaller tasks than a day are preferable). Effectively 80% to 90% tasks should be created in this planning meeting and put on the storyboard for anyone to pick up. There will be some unidentified tasks for sure, but that volume shouldn't be more than 10% to 20%, and those would be identified during the sprint period.

At the end of the Sprint Planning, the storyboard should be filled with newly created tasks with the status of "Not Started". Otherwise, it is an indication that the stories are not groomed enough or the team doesn't know what to do with that story. Either of them is not a good sign for a productive Agile team.

Deliver early and quickly

Agile is all about working software. So, it is pretty obvious to have continuous delivery of working software. I would like to emphasize it in light of Architectural components that usually take more time to build at the beginning of a project. But it is better to keep that working software concept even for the architectural components.

For example, if there's a framework to be built for workflow, messaging, enterprise integration, etc., it is better to plan to deliver the smallest piece of that working architectural component with minimal functional user stories (much like a Prototype but a working piece of software that would be the basis of further development). This is also aligned with the Lean concept of "fail fast and fail early" so that the recovery cost is low and manageable. Apart from early proof of concept, this task orientation also helps to rally the team around the delivery and gets the team in the performing stage quickly.

Track and remove impediments effectively

The Sprints are short. So, it is the responsibility of the organization to put a framework to track impediments and remove them as quickly as possible. The agility can't be achieved if the team is playing rat and mouse game with the organizational process instead of developing working software. It sounds easy and every organization will pledge to this principle immediately as soon as you ask for it but it is much bigger than just giving a pledge. The entire organization needs to be oriented to the Agile culture to serve an Agile team effectively.

Use visuals everywhere and anywhere

Human brains are not naturally built for reading lots of texts and interpreting the progress status of the team from the text is not even intuitive. Also, as Agile is like a fast-moving car running with the "pedal to the metal", the status of the team and product should be readable with a glimpse of an eye. So, keeping the status of Release and Sprint, in the form of a burn-down graph, in-front of eyes (or accessible with one click) is key. Every member of the team should be on the same page on where the team stands right at this moment.

Kanban Dashboard is another nice tool to visually track the progress of an Agile team. Just by a glimpse at the dashboard, one can paint the right picture of the team's current state.

Realize the self-organized team

It is easier said than done. Sometimes we don't even understand the breadth of the self-organization aspect of team management. Managing a self-organized team needs a whole new set of skill sets and attitudes that aren't easy for a traditionally trained manager. It would take another article to explain the management of a self-organized team but in a quick nutshell: it is like you tell the team to get things done by not just doing the "telling" thing.

Moreover, it is not that having a self-organized team is good to have but it is necessary to have the team self-organized due to the fact of business involvement and transparency in Agile. The analogy of the transparency is like you break the wall of the kitchen in your restaurant and allow the diners to come and talk to the chef and order their food while standing next to the cook in the kitchen. There's no place of "hide and seek" in an Agile team.

Scrum

Scrum is the most popular Agile software development methodology at this current moment. If you think in a purist sense, Scrum is more of a software project management framework than a software development methodology. But let's set that aside. Scrum has a lightweight process, roles, and ceremonies. There are tons of resources online about Scrum so you will get more than you would need from there and I will touch upon some of the building blocks of Scrum. At the very least, read the Scrum guide to start with *https://www.scrumguides.org/scrum-guide.html*. I will describe some of the basics from my point of view.

Scrum Team consists of primarily three roles: Product Owner, Scrum Master, and Developers. The Product Owner or PO is the business also known as the voice of the customer. The PO brings the vision to the team and works with the Scrum team to get that realized in small product increments. PO creates the Product Backlog, the list of User Stories ranked in a prioritized sequence. Scrum Master (SM) is the servant leader. SM owns the Scrum ceremonies and leads the team from behind. Apart from keeping disciplined and resolving impediments, SM should be very good at conflict resolution. Finally, the Developer role is dedicated to all the team members in the Scrum team. Developers understand the requirement, write the User Stories, implement and test those User Stories in the software, and finally deploy the product increment in the working software.

Scrum Ceremonies are promised to be lightweight and most of the cases they are true, however, the developer may still feel that those are a little too much especially for the Sprint planning. Without going much detail into that debate, let's quickly see the ceremonies. The Sprint (usually 2 to 4 weeks) starts with a Sprint Planning that goes from 4 to 8 hours depending on the length of the Sprint. In that planning working session, the detailed plan is created at the Tasks level for the next few weeks. After that team gets into the Daily Standup meeting that should be strictly not more than 15 minutes and asks three questions: What the developer had done since the team met, what the developer would do until the next meet up and finally, what, if any, is slowing the developer down. One thing to remember, the Daily Standup isn't a status meeting so refrain from asking status questions. This is also dubbed as "the Daily Planning" meeting. The other two ceremonies are slated for the end of the Sprint. The Sprint Review is to demo the working software product to the world. During this demo, PO shows off to the world what the team had done. The last ceremony is the Retrospective meeting where the team looks back to determine what went well, what didn't go well, and what the team would do differently in the next Sprint to improve - this is the continuous improvement tool for Scrum.

The primary artifacts of Scrum are User Story and Product Backlog. User Story captures the requirement from the perspective of a real user. The Product Backlog is the laundry list of User Stories ranked in the priority of the product's need combined with the potential business value. For more detail, read the chapter on Scrum.

Extreme Programming (XP)

Extreme Programming is to push the limit of the waterfall development process and do more fast-paced development with faster and predictive delivery by a small and highly motivated team. Most of the current best practices, such as unit testing, continuous integration, frequent code refactoring, frequent interactions with real users and review, etc. are the product of XP.

Learn more on XP: *https://en.wikipedia.org/wiki/Extreme_programming*.

Pair Programming

To describe Pair Programming in short: two programmers work on the same code while sharing one computer to write the code. While one programmer writes the code, the other programmer keeps looking at the

Chapter 5: Software Development Methodologies

code, inspecting it, suggesting it, and improving it instantly. Though this is a great way to develop software that would drastically reduce the bugs in the code as well as improve the quality of the code, very few companies' dares to afford it due to the perceived redundant cost. Apart from the quality of the code and product, this removes the tower of dependency where the knowledge is captivated by a few programmers in the team. I had once done pair programming to refactor (redesign to be exact) the most complex piece of code in the software that ended up with almost no bugs after the refactoring. However, for debugging code, Pair Programming is often used very effectively. Learn more about Pair programming on *https://en.wikipedia.org/wiki/Pair_programming*.

Test-Driven Development

Test-Driven Development or TDD is the method where the software development is done in the reverse traditional approach. The fundamental of TDD is to write the unit test code first before you write your actual software code but just a skeleton. Once your test code is developed and fails when executed, you then start putting meat into the skeleton to make them pass one at a time. This method is also part of Extreme Programming and getting momentum once again in the industry. Learn more about TDD on *https://en.wikipedia.org/wiki/Test-driven_development*.

Scaling Agile

Even though Agile is designed to deliver with small teams, as it became popular large enterprises have started identifying ways to implement it in large projects or programs.

Scaled Agile Framework (SAFe) and Spotify Model are two widely used scaled models for Agile development.

Scaled Agile Framework (SAFe)

As the name implies, this framework is designed to scale the Agile principles in an enterprise level structured through a synchronous body of knowledge. In its heart it defines a set of organizational and workflow patterns to promote alignment, collaboration, and delivery across multiple Agile teams. The downside of SAFe is that it is complex and to some extent - rigid. If you don't want to implement SAFe due to its

Chapter 5: Software Development Methodologies

complexity, I won't blame you for that. If you are interested in scaling our Agile development in your organization through SAFe, at least use the principles behind the SAFe model, if you don't want to take it to its entirety.

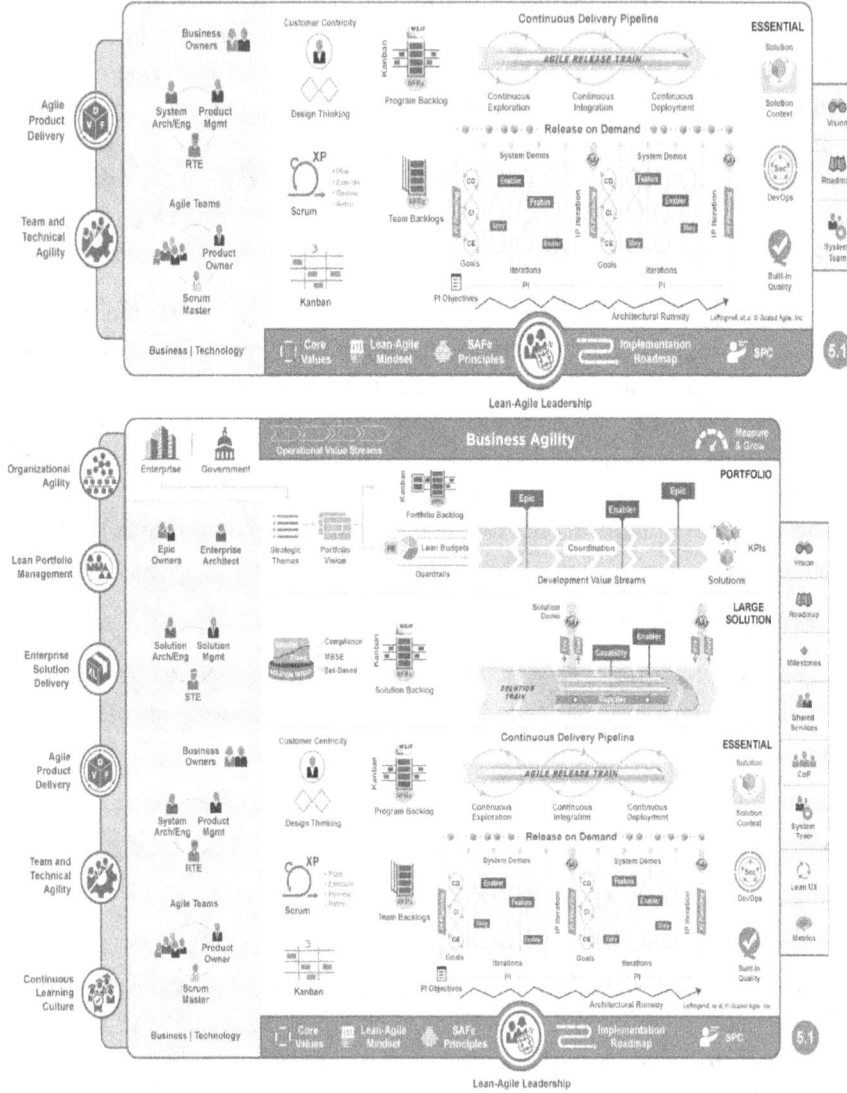

Figure-8: Essential SAFe[9] and Figure-9: Full SAFe[10]

Chapter 5: Software Development Methodologies

The SAFe principles are[10]:

- Principle #1 Take an economic view
- Principle #2 Apply systems thinking
- Principle #3 Assume variability; preserve options
- Principle #4 Build incrementally with fast, integrated learning cycles
- Principle #5 Base milestones on objective evaluation of working systems
- Principle #6 Visualize and limit Work in Process (WIP), reduce batch sizes, and manage queue lengths
- Principle #7 Apply cadence, synchronize with cross-domain planning
- Principle #8 Unlock the intrinsic motivation of knowledge workers
- Principle #9 Decentralize decision making
- Principle #10 Organize around value

Spotify Model

Scaling Agile at Spotify, the music streaming company, brought "the people" back to the center of the development methodology which was to some extent compromised in Scrum or other Agile methodologies. It gives back the autonomy to the people thus enabling it to scale at enterprise scale. Henrik Kniberg & Anders Ivarsson first published the whitepaper the Scaled Agile @ Spotify and this model took off like a storm[11].

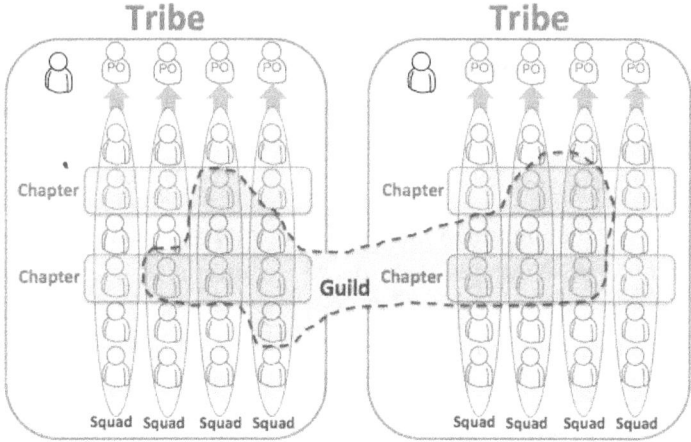

Figure-10: Spotify Model

The Spotify whitepaper has given a pretty neat and short walkthrough of the model but if you need even a shorter description, here you go.

The teams are called Squad which is a self-organized and autonomous organization that creates its structure that fits best for its value proposition. The Squads are organized into tribes that work in a related area in a coordinated manner. Tribes also run autonomously. To offset too much autonomy and prevent falling into anarchy, the Chapter and Guild are formed to bring synergy and "Matrix" style with functional management and collaboration.[12]

Hybrid SDLC

Hybrid approach is to use the Waterfall method's good old planning and then the dynamism of Agile methodology and combine them into one. Usually, every project manager or software development manager comes up with some sort of custom molded SDLC that can be called a Hybrid method. However, Project Management Institute (PMI) has also popularized the Disciplined Agile Delivery (DAD) which can also be denoted as Hybrid method to manage projects that mixes the waterfall method with Agile to exploit the best of both breeds. PMI has defined DAD as: Disciplined Agile® Delivery (DAD) is a people-first, learning-oriented hybrid agile approach to IT solution delivery. DAD addresses all aspects of the full delivery life cycle, supporting multiple ways of working (WoW) that can be tailored for the context that you face. DAD encompasses all aspects of agile software development in a robust, pragmatic, and governable manner.

Agile software development ignored (to be more accurate, assumed) the reality of enterprise outside of hardcore technical software development work. An example is - you never start a government agency software development by telling them that we don't know exactly what we are going to build, how long it will take to build and how much cost it would incur at the end of the software development. Agile assumes that all those are somehow taken care of and now the technical challenge has been dropped to the software professionals to build the solution. DAD or such kind of methods, I call them the Hybrid SDLC, which comes to bridge the gap of repeatable Systems implementation where there are less unknown and baseline requirements can be gathered and afterwards the variance changes are kept open during the implementation without making rigid assumptions on outside or inside of the software development technical endeavor. This approach can be applied in the government or regulatory projects where you would need to go through the traditional processes (e.g., RFP, Bidding, etc.) and meet other stringent formalities.

DAD and the mindset of it is nicely explained in this article:

https://www.pmi.org/disciplined-agile/process/introduction-to-dad/why

https://www.pmi.org/disciplined-agile/process/introduction-to-dad/mindset

Design Thinking

Now, you have seen many SDLC methodologies and you can pick the best fit for your organization and delivery. There's another concept, regardless of what SDLC you use, that focuses on how to solve the right problem for the users. This is known as the Human-Centered Design or Design Thinking. To understand that, let's walk into a hypothetical conference room where a hypothetical conversation is taking place between a software engineer and a business user:

"I need to have the development team available and ready twenty-four by seven during the filing period. This is Fed mandated SLA and we would have to react within 4 to 24 hours. If any approval is needed to do the immediate deployment to the production, secure the necessary management approval upfront." said the business user.

"Do you really need the development and production support team to sit at their desk and wait to jump in to reintegrate the financial models into the production environment? What problem are you trying to solve here? Are you looking for a way to have the changed models reintegrated into the production environment within a short period to meet the stringent Fed mandates SLA?" The software engineer replied with an empathic voice. Further, adding to it by proposing a potential solution to that problem, "How about we provide you a self-service capability to reintegrate the models into the production system? You can do that anytime you want it and any number of times you need it."

"That sounds interesting but I don't want anyone to change the production system anytime without proper approval", the business user reacted in a receptive tone.

"I don't want that either", the Software Engineering Manager is now chipping into the conversation, "We can enforce a four-eyes check but let's talk more about the details before we jump into the final solution", and has steered the discussion towards finding the right solution.

Though this may be a hypothetical conversation, certainly you have seen a similar conversation where the business user approaches the software engineering or product development team with a "brilliant" IT solution of a business problem without even mentioning what business problem the user was trying to solve. However, the goals of the software engineering team should be to steer the conversation towards understanding the users' pain points, find the fundamental problem, and then propose the right solution.

To me, that is the essence of Design Thinking!

Design Thinking is not the new guy in the town even though its reincarnation sounds just like that. I don't want to spend a whole lot about its historical aspect but let's put just enough history for the sake of giving a context.

Design Thinking as a concept came into existence in the late sixties when Herbert A. Simon published his book, "The science of the Artificials". This got into the mainstream through the establishment of Stanford University's Design School.

Before delving into the details of Design Thinking, let's first clarify, "what's Design?"

Design, though it sounds like the surface or outward appearance of a thing, however, this concept of design is furthest from that vain outward look and feel. IBM Design Thinking defines Design as "The Intent behind the outcome". But the most intricate definition of Design came from the man who had changed the way we perceive the computer products, Steve Jobs, who once said in his interview that the reason he doesn't like the Microsoft's product because "it doesn't have the taste", and defined Design as "...the fundamental soul of a man-made creation that ends up expressing itself in successive outer layers". And Design Thinking is the art of creation of Design.

Now, let's take the words from two other most influential persons who have helped the Design Thinking to come to its current state: Don Norman, the author of "The Design of Everyday Things", has described the Design Thinking as "...Designers resist the temptation to jump immediately to a solution for the stated problem. Instead, they first spend time determining what basic fundamental (root) issue needs to be addressed. They don't try to search for a solution until they have determined the real problem, and even then, instead of solving that problem, they stop to consider a wide range of potential solutions. Only then will they finally converge upon their proposal. This process is called design thinking." Tom Brown, the founder of IDEO, has defined Design Thinking as "...a human-centered approach to innovation that draws from the designer's toolkit to integrate the needs of people, the possibilities of technology, and requirements for business success".

Now, the question would come to your mind that if we can capture that art into our practice and if possible, how. The answer is yes, it can be taught to an extent. I would argue that this skill just can't be learned, it has to be acquired. The foundation of Design Thinking lies in empathy and observation. If you have those, you can thrive in Design Thinking but if you don't have those, you can learn it to survive. Here's a very brief list of few tools and techniques to practice Design Thinking:

Empathy: you have to have empathy for the user of the software product that you're creating. Put yourself into their shoes, feel their urges and pains. Understand what they say, what they feel, what they think, and what they do.

Observation: observe your users and customers in their setting. Don't invite them to a meeting room and ask them what they want. Go to their place and observe what they do. Don Norman in his The Design of Everyday Things book went so far into that he suggested to "Watch them into their homes, schools, and office. Watch them commute, at parties, at mealtime, and with friends at the local bar. Follow them into the shower if necessary, because it is essential to understand the real situations that they encounter, not some pure isolated experience."

Persona: this is the archetype of your software users. Understand the personas not only as a user but also as a human. Use observation techniques to recognize the personas.

Continuous Feedback: get frequent feedback from your users. This is very much aligned with the Agile concept. Don't just assume that you're building the right product but do a frequent show and tell. Have your users feel your product. Let them touch and feel it. Use validated learning to continuously improve your product.

Myths and truths of collocation

All the Agile and Design Thinking ideas go around the highly interactive environment in a collocated area that brings the best of collaboration. I am also an Agile advocate and don't doubt the benefit of collocation. The collocation doesn't just dramatically reduce the communication cost in the team but also helps tremendously to avoid confusion and improve team bonding. This is becoming a norm in software development work where agility is a new buzzword in the town. But how this collocation is implemented is more important than just cramming people into a giant blob of space which can do more harm than benefit for the software development team.

Traditionally, the large non-software development enterprises are not designed for collocating software developers in a common space. So, when they are asked by their Software development department to create space, for instance, for their Agile software development team, the people

Chapter 5: Software Development Methodologies

from the reality department free up a big enough conference room that can "just fit" the entire team. The expectation is, now the team would start producing the fruits of collocation. Quite a few things are missing in this expectation. Let's check them one by one:

- Those (just freed up) conference rooms are built and organized for face-to-face communication in a meeting setting. A meeting is expected to run in terms of minutes, not hours. So, there may not be enough space to place the computer on the table, chairs are not healthy enough for day-long seating, not enough lights and ventilation for 10 to 15 people and the list continues.
- A team is composed of people and people have certain biological and psychological needs. People need enough legroom, yawning space, etc. without bumping into each other. Except for a few people, most of the people need off-facetime. Otherwise, the side effects of 24/7 cable news channels pop up.
- Creativity needs both the conscious and subconscious minds to tango. With only the conscious mind in play, only so much can be achieved but to come up with a good idea and solutionize that idea, the subconscious mind needs to be triggered which needs a relatively quiet and private space. This is true for a software programmer. They need interaction with other fellow programmers to discuss and bring new ideas and then go back to relative isolation to concretely think through that idea to make it work. In lack of that, you will see people are putting on their earbuds to cancel the surrounding noise where no physical isolation is available.
- Believe it or not, people can't work, especially people who are in a creative business-like software development, continuously for hours after hours without breaking away from that monotone. It works in a certain situation and setting but the majority time it needs a social break. So, if we force people to be in the crowd all the time, we may get lines of code that just do the work but not a breakthrough solution that will lower the total cost of software development and maintenance.

- I am not necessarily suggesting that people need to be a mile apart from each other but at the very least we need to recognize the need of balancing the collocation with personal space to get the best out of collocation.

CHAPTER VI

Chapter 6: Software Design Review

Chapter 6: Software Design Review

Regardless of the Software Project Management style your organization follows or the SDLC methodology is chosen, the software development should have a technical design and review process. Hearing the term "process" developers may start to despise it without even trying it. I understand that there are justifications behind that "process-trauma". Most of the time this kind of processes are done by government agencies and those are horrendously complex and to some extent "non-sense". Those were also done mostly when the SDLC were dominated by the "Waterfall" method. However, as most of the SDLC methodologies now are either Agile or Agile-like, those rigid, complex processes should have no way to be returned. Completely agree with that mindset. Thus, the Design Review process should also be done completely in Agile mode. As a manager, most probably you will be a Design Reviewer (or approver, depending on the organization's structure and size), however, you may also play the role of the Architect if your team is small and it doesn't have one. Nonetheless, having a deep understanding of the process is critical for you to ensure your software delivery organization can repeatedly produce quality software.

Here's a simple depiction of a Design Review process.

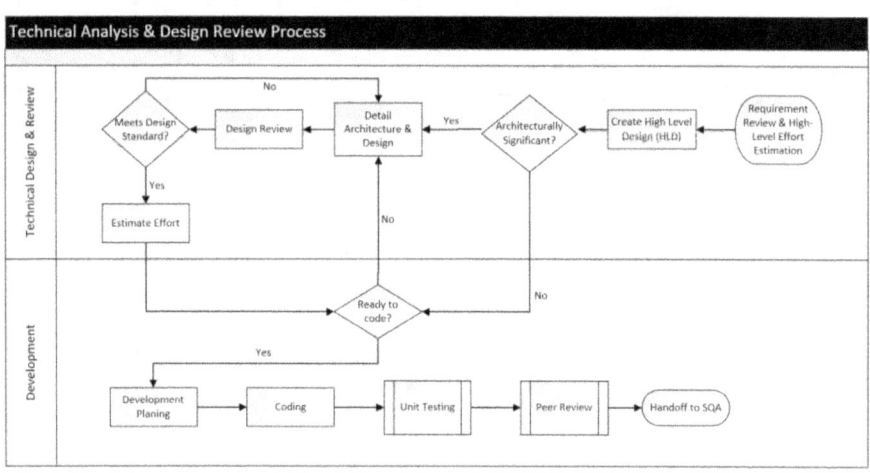

Figure-11: Software Design Review Process

Requirement Review & High-Level Effort Estimation

The design process starts at the Requirement. The requirement is analyzed and clarified before the design process even starts. Remember the concept GIGO: Garbage-In-Garbage-Out. So, to have a quality design and a software, you need a quality requirement. At this stage you review if the software requirement is complete to estimate the effort to build the software. Also, during this time, usually the effort estimation is done at a very high-level using T-shirt sizing, Fibonacci numbering etc. with higher margin of error. Refer to the "Cone of uncertainty" in the Software Requirement Management & Cost Estimation chapter for more detail on how to do software estimation.

Create a very High-Level Design (HLD)

The goal of the design should be to convey the "intent" of the solution implementation to the reviewer before starting the implementation. Create a bird's-eye level solution design that can be progressively elaborated to further detail as needed. Prefer minimalistic approach over comprehensiveness: do not add more than what's needed to convey the solution design. If a sketch diagram conveys the intent, use that. If a few sentences are good enough to explain it, that's perfectly ok. Rely on your technical judgment and be confident in your judgment.

Is it an Architecturally Significant Requirement (ASR)?

Not all requirements (User Story/Defect) need Architecture & Design analysis. The requirement should be considered as an ASR, when it is to, as for instance:

- Implement a new large functionality.
- Changing an existing functionality that's going to impact the current systems architecture
- Adding significant changes to Design & implementation (new tools/library).
- Have non-functional impacts like Security, Performance, Availability, Testability, etc.

- For other changes like, changing the public interface of API, changing data model (adding/dropping columns or tables, adding Views, changing relationship), changing a class/method that has high dependency by other class/method, changes in the UI and UX that would impact customers, etc.

If the above list is true for your changes, use the Detail Architect & Design and subsequently the Design Review processes, otherwise you can skip and go directly into the Development planning and coding stage.

Detail Architecture & Design

At this stage, the HLD is elaborated to cover in greater detail as this requirement has potential impact in the overall architecture of the solution. There are few important aspects of software design that should be covered:

- Summary analysis of the functional and non-functional requirements, such as, technical specifications, assumptions made for the solution, alternate solutions that are analyzed and the proposed solution that best fit the requirement.
- The Functional Systems Design such as Process Design, External systems integration, Data Model design, data migration and transformation, etc.
- The Non-Functional Systems Design should contain the software quality attributes, such as Security, Performance, Scalability, Testability, and development efficiency.
- Development and Deployment Topology may contain development tech stack, production & Disaster Recovery topology, etc.

Design Review

In the review, let the developer or architect who designed the solution, explain the solution to the reviewer(s). The reviewer should ensure that the design meets the requirements and software quality attributes. The *Design Review Schedule* should be defined i.e., agreed up and documented, even if the organization prefers ad-hoc reviews. Also, try to synchronize the design review with the SDLC cadence, e.g., Scrum cadence like Sprint and Release schedules.

A sample Design Review process:

- Developers create the solution design and send it to Design for review.
- Design reviewer provides the feedback and decision to go ahead and implement the solution
- If it requires more information or has significant concerns, then the Design reviewer can trigger the formal review meeting and provide the recommendation/approval afterwards.
- If any deviation is needed during the implementation, that should be notified to the Design Reviewer and follow the Design Review process as needed

Even though the next steps are not specific to Design Review, as a manager, it's useful to know the basics of the next stages of development. Details of that are covered in the chapters: Software Development Methodologies and Deep Dive into Agile Scrum.

Development Planning is done using the organization's preferred SDLC (refer to the chapter: Deep Dive into Agile for more detail). During coding, use the Clean Code principle: "Always leave the code better than you found it". Additionally, make sure the technical debts are managed in the SDLC.

In some cases, it may not be practical to meet all non-functional quality attributes due to reasons such as urgent functional delivery, limited development resources, or hard deadlines. In such unique circumstances, it's important to document the technical debt and move forward. However, it's crucial to note that technical debt should never be used as an excuse to ship products with functional bugs.

Unit Testing should be part of the SDLC strategy and passed as a criteria of code completion. There are many benefits of unit testing: speed in development and confidence in changing code anytime. It allows the developers to change the code confidently without worrying if the change is breaking something that is unintended. This is also the remedy of the symptom where "if the code is working don't touch that due to the fear of breaking". However, that's only feasible when we reach a certain threshold of Unit Testing coverage. There's no magic number but usually 80% Unit Test coverage of the code is the point where Unit Test codebase starts to show the benefit and you can change/refactor the overall codebase confidently without fear.

Use a formal *Peer-Review* process for every change. Use the tool as much as possible (e.g., Git Pull Request and SonarQube code scan). The peer reviewer should ensure the organizational guidelines for development and coding are met. The unit test coverage, coding standard scan, security scan, non-functional requirement test results are reviewed as part of the review.

CHAPTER VII

Chapter 7: Deep Dive into Agile Scrum

As a Software Development Manager, you should have a deep understanding of at least one of the SDLC methodology used to develop software. What other than Scrum can fit in that bill? Scrum is the most successful implementation of Agile philosophy among the range of Agile software development methodologies available to date. To be more accurate, Scrum has combined the software project management aspect into the Agile SDLC and upheld the Agile manifesto to its best. In the first two editions of the book, I consciously decided not to add many details of Agile Scrum and how to build a Scrum team. However, my years of experience managing the Agile team has revealed that though this is the most popular and widely used development methodology, people often use the tools and techniques of Scrum without truly appreciating the philosophy behind each of the Scrum fundamentals. In this section, you will find the focus mostly on the "why" of the Scrum process rather than the "what" of that. The lack of that understanding and appreciation of the Scrum philosophy creates an environment where team members apparently use the Scrum but are not able to realize the promise of it and, to its worst, the team even sometimes not able to fathom the gap of its implementation. Also, Scrum demands all the parties to go through a behavioral transformational journey which is the primary reason why Scrum is, according to the Scrum Guide, "Easy to understand but difficult to master." Truly speaking, it's not that Scrum is the only methodology that would produce you working software - there are other Iterative methodologies out there that produce a large amount of software so it's not that you would have no other choice. So, if you wish to go with another methodology, go for it, however, considering the effectiveness and transparency, Scrum is by far the best software development methodology available at your disposal.

If you are completely new to Scrum, I strongly recommend reading the Scrum Guide[15] to get the standard understanding of it. Once you read through the guide, you would get all the "what" and some of the "why" and finally mesh it up with this section to reach your goal. Reiterating the focus by taking the warning sign in the Scrum guide - "it's easy to

Chapter 7: Deep Dive into Agile Scrum

understand the Scrum but difficult to master it", this chapter would focus on how to "master it".

SCRUM FRAMEWORK

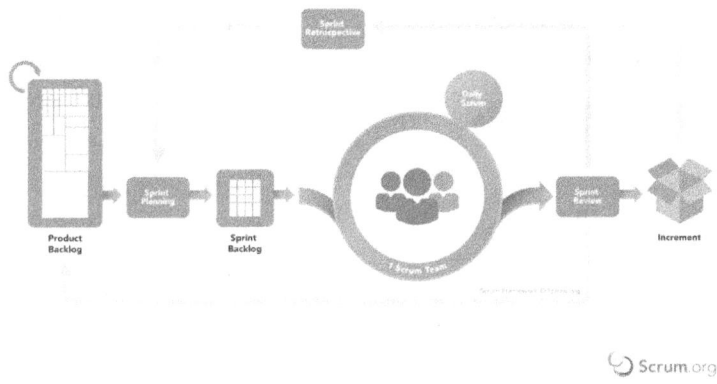

Figure-12: SCRUM Framework[16]

How (and why) to build a Scrum team

People

The first step of building an Agile team is to hire the skilled members for the most critical three roles: Developer, Scrum Master, and Product Owner.

Developers are the engine of the Scrum team. Though the term Developer sounds the same as for any other software development team, however, within a true Scrum team the Developer is more than just a developer in a traditional sense. The Scrum developer needs to be skilled in multiple roles that are brought under the umbrella of this title: Analyst, QA, DevOps, and, albeit, Developer. The person needs to be able to change the hat from time to time to play that particular skill: play the role of QA engineer when testing another developer's code, as an Analyst to gather detailed requirements from the form of User Stories. On top of that, the very nature of Agile is agility which means the team should be ready to embrace any change. This would lead to work on new tools and technologies in a short period. So, the interview process of hiring a Scrum developer would be very different from the traditional development team. Look for the below traits in that person:

- Brevity and Clarity: strong communication skills i.e., ability to articulate a problem statement and the solution of it in concise and clear words. Among all other needs, these traits are required to understand and communicate to analyze user stories. Apart from all other reasons, the Daily Scrum is for just 15 minutes and having people who love to explain everything or who can't explain things in short and to the point, will hurt the entire team's productivity.
- Prefer the developer who has the breadth of the software development (having at least one specialization) over depth alone. Don't make the mistake of hiring a jack of all trades alone as that will lead your team towards a team of talkers rather than a team of doers. The developer should be an "expert" in at least one area along with all other skill sets. That would be a testimony that that developer can go deep into solving a problem and can learn the other things when needed.
- Hire the learner - preferably a lifelong learner. It's not just learning when needed, it should be learning for the sake of learning and using that new learning in the next software solution the team would work on. If the learning is always to solve a specific problem, which is required, but when the learning is horizontally spread, the groundbreaking idea and solution may come out through it. Steve Jobs had taken a Calligraphy course, just for the sake of learning, during his college dropout period and, in his word, the Macintosh wouldn't come with that groundbreaking variable spaced fonts had he not taken that course years ago without even knowing if that learning would be of any use in his life.
- Mix your team with Analytic skills and non-Analytic (such as Intuition) skills. Though the intuition may sound wishy-washy but never discount the strength of intuition. However, the intuition has to come

from a person with enough experience in that field (as a rule of thumb: it takes roughly 10 years to grow wisdom in a particular area).
- Look for genuinely curious minds. The person who is not curious about why something is done in a certain way, can't come up with genuine ideas.
- Finally, make sure that the person's aptitude doesn't get skewed into one area too much over the others as that may lead to many unintended consequences and unpleasant team experience. It will be like a vehicle, where all the wheels aren't inflated properly to move forward straight, and having one tire extremely deflated or inflated would take your car to a tangent that, if not balanced, would lead towards an undesired direction.

Team Building

Team building in Scrum is not very different from any other team building. The goal may differ in some cases but all other standard team-building artifacts and processes can be followed. There're books and literature on Team Building discipline that can be applied here. Whatever you do otherwise, make sure to focus on shortening the two "ing": Storming and Norming of five stages of Team Building (i.e., Forming, Norming, Storming, Performing and Adjourning). People set aside personal conflicts at individual levels when there's an overarching goal that acts as a North Star during the Storming and Norming stages.

Scrum Team Roles

Product Owner

PO is rather the most simplistic, however, the anchor role among the other Scrum roles. PO carries the vision of the product being built. In terms of authority, PO enjoys the most dictating role and the only point of decision making for the product being built. The authority comes in the form of owning decisively the Product Backlog. The demarcation of the ownership has to be crystal clear - PO owns the Product Backlog, not the Scrum Team. That's the behavioral transformation Scrum demands a PO to go through. It sounds simpler but practicing it is difficult. The analogy of this balancing act can be understood by the balance of power among the US government's branches- Executive branch and Legislative branch. The legislative branch owns the lawmaking and the Executive branch enforces that law. Without having both branches work hand in hand, the government would be paralyzed and not achieve the goal of governance.

Scrum Master (SM)

SM is the Servant leader who needs to play both Autocratic and Democratic processes in different settings. Autocratic for Scrum Events, Ceremonies, and Scrum set rules. SM is the protector of the team from external influence during the Sprint. The success or failure of an SM can be gauged by the state of "Self-organization" within the team. You can put a scale of one to ten and measure it. Now the question is why "self-organization" is so critical for SM to nurture? The answer is – because Scrum isn't hierarchical but a flat organization. The team should own the product delivery. If the team doesn't become self-organized, then the true benefit of Agile can't be reaped. This is explained in much detail in the previous chapter.

So, how do you know that the team has reached the state of self-organization? Do this litmus test: if the SM can't take a vacation for two weeks without impacting the velocity of the Sprint, SM has failed in his or her job.

Developer

Developers are the key part of any software development team, but when it comes to Scrum, they are the heart and soul of it. I have alluded to their competences, attitude, and aptitude in the prior section. If you want to label them in one word, they are the "Ninja" in the team - they would not be just a technical geek but a process geek as well. If you fail with them, you are failing the Scrum. The other two roles: SM and PO, are key roles as well but they are much easier to fill and replace. To be fair, all the spotlights are constantly on them - starting from the Sprint Planning through Sprint Demo. It may not be an exaggeration to say that all other roles and artifacts are to aid them to be successful so that the Scrum is successful. Developers play the role of Analyst when grooming the Product Backlog, understanding the requirement i.e., "what to build" through accepting the User Story, plan the development work by creating the Tasks to achieve the User Story goal according to the Acceptance Criteria, design the software, do the coding, test the software, and finally deploy (through DevOps) the working software to the Production environment. What is left in this process? Now you must appreciate why they are the heart of the Scrum. The Scrum hates the procrastinators - this came to declare the end of it. Many developers enjoy procrastination and working through the night before the build which is often considered as heroic. To be a good Scrum citizen, developers have to change that mindset - which is the biggest and maybe the only obstacle (apart from doing the development planning early enough in terms of Tasks) to master the Scrum.

How would you know that the developer is the right fit for the Scrum team? Do this litmus test: if Developers are assigned the Tasks in the Sprint rather than pull it from the Task board, they are not ready for Scrum yet.

Scrum Artifacts

User Story

User Story is a very simple and straightforward concept in Scrum. The balancing of the "Collaboration over contract" manifestation is done through this Scrum artifact. The User Story is the contract between the PO and Developers. As mentioned in the Scrum Guide, the User Story has to define "what to build " rather "how to build" and control the outcome of the build through the "Acceptance Criteria". As a warning to all who thinks writing user story is easy (yes, it's very easy for who has mastered it), I have seen people writing user story for years but can't get out of that "what" vs. "how" conflicts due to the mentality of waterfall fashion "BRD" or "FSD". The most difficult part of a user story is to create a smaller story that will fit within Sprint. If it doesn't fit, it has to split - and that's an art of splitting the user story.

User Story Task

Though Task doesn't earn the status of independent top-level artifacts, however, I would add this as a top-level artifact (albeit under the purview of User Story) due to its importance and significance to achieve a repeatable software development outcome.

I spend most of my time to explaining Scrum teams, repeatedly, the power of breaking down the User Story in terms of small enough Tasks: A Task that takes 4 hours or less to complete is desirable; a Task that takes between 4 - 8 hours to complete is OK; if it takes more than 8 hours then it needs be broken down into smaller Tasks. And I amazingly find out that Task is the single thing which is misunderstood the most or ineffectively used by the Scrum Team. There are many best practices to create Tasks and I would touch upon a few of the most important ones but let's first understand the philosophy behind the importance of Tasks.

As you have already known, a User Story is written from the user's perspective and defines "what" the user wants the system to do. There'd be nothing on a specific technology (unless it's so obvious like it's a GUI, for instance), solution, etc. Task plays that pivotal role and forces Developers to create a micro-Development plan for that user story. To put into the context: Tasks would be the outcome of the team's micro-planning of a User Story within the Sprint planning. Few things to remember in creating Tasks:

- Tasks should be created by the entire team - no playing in isolation. Every developer would create Tasks and understand each Task as if he or she would complete it individually.
- Tasks would be owned by a Developer - not the complete User Story. This is where individual ownership meshes up with Teamwork. In the Daily Scrum, developers would talk about the Tasks for a User Story to demonstrate individual ownership. As Developers complete the Tasks and the completion of User Story needs multiple developers to

Chapter 7: Deep Dive into Agile Scrum

complete their Tasks, this creates the team spirit and curves out all the negativity of selfishness of individuality. The User Story is owned by the team and Scrum Master is the custodian of the User Story and ensures the completion of all the Tasks by the Developers.

- Tasks aren't assigned to Developers by SM or others rather Developers assign the tasks to themselves. Otherwise, as mentioned earlier, it would break the very essence of the Self-organization aspect of the team. Agile is all about the ownership and when you're assigning it to a developer by SM, you're hitting the very fundamentals of that philosophy hard.
- As mentioned, the goal of the Scrum team should be to create 80% of Tasks created during the Sprint Planning which would show that the team has a good grip on the technology and software solutions.

There are so many ways to create tasks, but here are few prescribed forms - don't be confined to it - use whatever way you see it fits the need of your team's skill set while fulfilling the purpose and philosophy of Tasks.

- By Layer: you can create tasks of User Interface, Business logic, Data logic, API creation, etc.
- By Technology: you can create tasks by technology skills, like Java, Python, REST service, JavaScript, Spark, SQL, Hadoop, AWS, Unix, etc.
- By Component: you can create the task of each component of your software architecture (clue: each box in the Architecture's Box diagram)

How would you know that the Tasks are created right? Do this litmus test: measure the number of new Tasks created during the Sprint and the threshold should be 20%. Above that percentage, the team isn't doing the job right.

Product Backlog (PB)

PB is the laundry list of Items (in the form of Epic and User Story) that the PO wants from the team. Apart from the PB Items (PBI), the other two interesting things about the PB are that the list is organized into a ranked list that denotes the priority of a PBI in comparison to the rest. This artifact aids the transparency dimension of the Scrum. There should be nothing the team would work on that's not in the PB. This may sound so rational however you would see in a non-Agile environment (as long as in teams, where Agile isn't followed) there would be work items the team is working on and nobody would know where it came from. Another important aspect rather than a relationship of PB to PO: PO owns the Product Backlog and not the Scrum Team. The only leverage PO would have in the team is to set the priority of the PBI and natural progression into the Sprint Backlog based on the priority. PO's authority should strictly be contained within that area so that the team has the freedom to work during the Sprint with their full creativity. Otherwise, the core of Scrum value "Self-organization" would be a farfetched dream.

How would you know that the Product Backlog is in good health? Do this litmus test: a good PB would have 2 to 3 Sprint worth of User Stories in the ready-to-take state for the team to pick up in the Sprint Backlog. Also, if a User Story is added to the Sprint Backlog directly without going through the PO, it's a red flag that PO isn't maintaining the PB well.

Sprint Backlog

It's a subset of the PB which is owned by the Scrum team. Here PO is off-limits. The team's commitment manifests through the Sprint Backlog. Once the Sprint Backlog is created, the team would work to burn the stories down. Upholding the team's sovereignty on the Sprint Backlog during the Sprint is critical to nurture and sustain the self-organization, creativity, and ownership mindset. In exceptional cases, PO can request to add User Stories into the Sprint Backlog however that has to be agreed upon by the Developers, and PO should be ready to do a trade-off with other already committed user stories.

Definition of Ready (DoR)

Though Scrum, or to be more accurate, Agile does prefer collaboration over contracts, the DoR is one of the two contracts (the other one is the DoD: Definition of Done) that should be in place to keep away disputes during the Sprint. The beauty of the DoR is that this doesn't need to be a complicated legal document, instead, this is an agreed-upon statement

Chapter 7: Deep Dive into Agile Scrum

that the entire team comes up with and the PO would respect this contract when a User Story is to be taken into a Sprint. Some of the example clauses in the DoR could be:

- User Story is refined and sized by the Agile team.
- User story doesn't have any open impediment.
- User Story complies with the INVEST: Independent, Negotiable, Valuable, Estimable, Small enough, Testable criteria.

Definition of Done (DoD)

This is the other leg of the contract that should be hanging on every Scrum team's wall. Like the DoR, the DoD is the agreement in the Agile team that would be checked to verify if the User Story can be marked as completed. Though it sounds so trivial by most of the team that they often ignore this but this is vital for a conflict-free team. One can argue that the acceptance criteria of a User Story should have that DoD embedded. That absolutely can be done. However, the reason for taking out this team-wide (global) scope of acceptance criteria is to avoid repetitions of the same thing in every User Stories. Some of the example statements in the DoD could be:

- The Software should be tested and working in the SQA region.
- User Story should have all the underlying Tasks peer-reviewed and completed.

Burndown chart

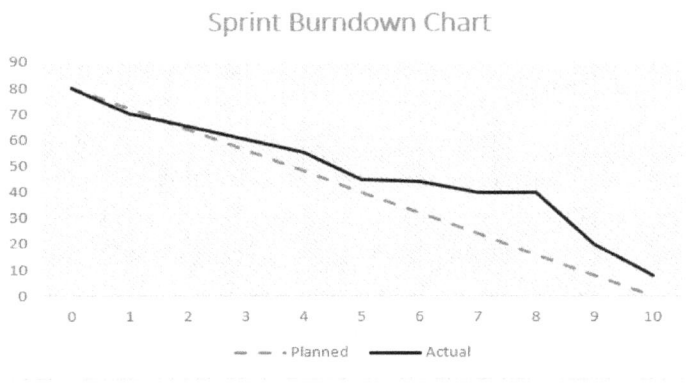

Figure-13: Burn-down chart[17]

Use this artifact effectively to bring the team on the same page to show the overall progress of the Sprint. If the Burn-down graph is not moving fast enough then the team should course correct. To understand why this is an effective artifact, you need to understand the power of making information public. The power of burn-down charts isn't because it's a cool looking graph but its power comes due to the power of visualization. You can simply write down the number of user story points that have been burned up and show the remaining points, however, that wouldn't create a similar vivid reality effect on the human brain compared to when it's shown in a graph. The human brain is built for visual processing and reacts to it instantly. Otherwise, you need to create the effect of numbers by processing that first and converting it into some kind of visuals.

Sprint Velocity

The empirical data is the driver behind the Agile Team's continuous improvement mantra. And Sprint Velocity creates the number one empirical data point that tells the team, and the other stakeholders, how the team is performing. Velocity is used to predict the team's capacity in upcoming Sprints. Keeping in line with overall Scrum management principles, the visualization is the key and this Velocity data would be a simple graph showing the total user story points delivered in a Sprint. Apart from other usages, the most important usage of this is during the Sprint planning (or overall Product Release planning) to forecast how long it may take to deliver working software.

Scrum Cadence

The goal of the Scrum cadence is to Burn-down the Sprint backlog, not the team. Understanding the cadence and the philosophy behind each Scrum event is crucial. I have seen teams using every Scrum event religiously but don't achieve the goal of a Scrum Team - a self-organized team due to the lack of appreciation and understanding the purpose of it. Hence, let's understand the events and their inherent purpose so that you realize the equilibrium between a self-organized and an independent Agile Scrum team that owns the outcome of the Scrum - the software solution.

Sprint

According to the Scrum Guide, a Sprint should be of 2-4 weeks based on the team size, software complexity, and team's capability. The lower the duration is the lesser the chance of waste is. I would suggest starting in the higher range with a brand-new team and settling to a smaller duration after a few sprints. The question is why a sprint should be smaller in duration compared to weeks or months of a development cycle. Like other cadence and artifacts, the answer lies in human psychology. Accept it or not, the human brain can't have a detailed plan in advance with full grip for more than a couple or a few weeks. If you go beyond 3 or 4 weeks, you start losing the details of the work to be done. Because Scrum demands the full commitment and complete grip of the Sprint by every developer in the team, nothing should be unknown, unclear, or unplanned about every user story on the day one of the Sprint. That'd be only possible if you keep the Sprint short enough to keep it in your head. An analogy of it is - programmers run an inbuilt compiler and executer in debug mode (like you have in any IDE) in their head. When they code or do modifications in the code, they compile and run the code in debug mode in their head to foresee the outcome. That's why you see most programmers (except a very few geniuses) work one piece of code at a time to avoid the cost of context switching. The context switching is like unloading the currently running code in the head and loading it in there. As Sprint is all about building a small increment of the software, it needs that level of clarity and grip for the Sprint cycle.

Product Backlog Grooming

The product backlog grooming has two purposes in the overall life of a Scrum team: refine the user stories to make it ready for the team to pick up in the Sprints. The key in the grooming session that distinguishes Scrum over other methodologies is - the entire team participates in the backlog grooming session. The PO would explain the User Stories to developers. They would analyze the user story and ask questions to clarify it. The team would allocate a certain percentage of the Sprint time for this cadence.

How would you know that this event is working? Do this litmus test: any less than 2 to 3 Sprint worth of fully ready User Stories in the PB indicates either the PB Grooming time allocation is inadequate or not effective due to the lack of team's skill and capabilities.

Sprint Planning

To some people who don't truly appreciate the philosophy of Scrum methodology, Scrum is synonymous with no or little planning. However, this is far from the truth. Scrum never preaches for no or little planning. In contrast, Scrum suggests more planning - to be more accurate - more frequent planning. If your Sprint's length is 2 - 4 weeks, you are planning for that duration. You don't put the entire product backlog on the table. This Sprint Planning is one planning event but the Product Owner (PO) would continuously do the planning for the product being built using Affinity sizing, Backlog grooming, etc. Nobody would question a roadmap of the product that the PO would have for the team; however, contrary to the Waterfall method, the PO can't take that to the stakeholder and claim that the team would certainly deliver this by a certain period. Nonetheless, PO needs to get some sort of high-level timeline to secure the budget for the team. That's why Scrum demands the PO is fully available and embedded in the team. The reason why Scrum leaves that overall roadmap planning outside of the Scrum team is because this would not just be a disservice to the developers to ask for what would happen in 6 months down the line when the detail of that isn't clearly understood. People may claim otherwise but for a human brain keeping a "very detailed" plan for more than 3-4 weeks is unrealistic. The "very detail" is meant for truly very detail. The Scrum team would have every detail of it including how to do it effectively - the creation of Tasks is a testament of that very detailed understanding. I have mentioned that in another section of this chapter.

The goal of the Sprint planning is to spend enough time (usually 4 hours for two weeks Sprint) for the team to ask questions to the PO if there's anything more, they need to clarify at the last moment and populate the Task Board with detail level Tasks. The Tasks should be small enough to complete in a few hours by a developer. As mentioned earlier, if you find new Tasks are created during the Sprint and that exceeds the 20% threshold, either the team doesn't have a full understanding of the product they are developing or they aren't skilled enough to do that planning. None of them would give any comfort to the PO.

Daily Scrum

This is the most used and abused Scrum event that you would come across in a lot of established Scrum teams. I have seen teams even after running for a year that they haven't mastered the use of the Daily Scrum meeting. Let's first understand the purpose of the Daily Scrum. This is the daily planning for the team - you will find that in Scrum guide and everyone agrees to it but why the Scrum has created three specific questions and strict brief meeting time (typically 15 minutes or less) - the answer to it will reveal the true purpose of it. The Daily Scrum achieves below things in just a few minutes:

- It takes each team member into the power of the individual ownership model. Scrum is all about the team but if you are covered under a team, there would be areas that won't be visible to all. There will be people who would wing it on others - that tendency would be unearthed during this call. If one team member is super busy and another one is just passing the time, and in the end, we equally distribute the fame and blame to both, that injustice would slowly but surely create a toxic environment. You would have to nip it at the bud - the Daily Scrum is that "magic" tool to identify it. The beauty of Scrum is that it magically binds the Team spirit to individual ownership which makes Scrum unique in the industry.

- It creates transparency to the team on who is doing what. That transparency is very crucial to create trust. Everyone in the team would know who is doing what. In this way, there won't be any information gap. If two developers are doing the same tasks by mistake or one developer is doing something that shouldn't be done, or should be done in a different way - this is the open forum to identify it.

Chapter 7: Deep Dive into Agile Scrum

- When developers give out the report of what task was done yesterday, other team members, including the Scrum Master would listen to it and get the feeling of progress. If someone is giving out the same status day after day, SM and other team members would pitch in to help out to expedite that area of development.
- The great part of it is to tell the "world" if anything is slowing them down. This is the single most cause why Scrum is fast - wickedly fast. A developer shouldn't wait more than a few hours before announcing to the world that she is stuck. Usually, developers are optimistic and want to solve the problem by themselves which can kill hours if not days before someone else even gets to know about it. The Daily Scrum ensures that in the worst case, the developer can't lose more than a day.
- It cuts the excess fat of status reporting from the team to the management. Anyone wants to know what's being done in the team, what the health of the team is, and how the team is doing it; they should just join the Daily Scrum. The transparency aspect of Scrum creates extra pressure to the team member in the beginning when the Agile mindset isn't fully installed but over the period and with the safety of self-organization, both the team and the management should feel comfortable that every one of the team members and stakeholders is doing everything possible for the success of the project goal.

Scrum Demo or Scrum Review

Contrary to all other Scrum events, the attendees of this event are all the stakeholders of the project. The senior in the rank shows up in the Demo the better for the team. The purpose of this event is to show the world the achievement of the Scrum team and its last Sprint. This will justify the money spent on this product and team over other competing products and teams. Believe it or not, at a certain point in time, every organization has competing priorities, just like your home improvement project - you have to make a trade-off. This is the time to create credentials and build team branding. Incorrectly, some teams keep User Story for this final day to show it to the PO in a ceremonial fashion but that doesn't justify the purpose of this event. It's more for the PO to show the cool functionality the team has built and how the team has made progress towards the product vision.

It's mentioned earlier but worth mentioning it again - close a User Story as soon as all the tasks are completed. Otherwise, how would you get the Burn-down chart in a nice steady downward linear graph? There may be one or a few User Stories that's not completed yet but try to complete it at least before the demo and get them closed ahead of time. This can also be considered as a sign that the Scrum team doesn't have a full grip on the technology, skill, scope, etc.

Scrum Retrospective

Retro is the Kaizen, the continuous improvement tool, for Scrum. In the Retro you allow everyone to speak freely and come up with three things: (a) what worked well in the last Sprint, (b) what didn't work well, and (c) what could be done differently. The team should agree to continue with the items in the list 'a' and to stop doing with the list 'b'. The list 'c' would give you to change the team's way of doing in the subsequent Sprint. From that list, pick the top 3 (voted by the team) action items to try out. Remember, Scrum is always in an experiment - so instead of spending more time debating whether that new approach would work or not, try it out for the next couple of weeks. If it works, keep it as part of the team norm, otherwise, trim it. This is the beauty of Scrum - no more speculative assumption and analysis paralysis - try it out before you make a big investment into it.

Scrum pre-requisites

Continuous Integration and Continuous Delivery (CI/CD) mantra of DevOps is not just important for Scrum but is the foundation for Scrum success. No amount of polishing in Scrum roles, Scrum artifacts, or Scrum Processes would create the fruit of it unless you have built a CI/CD in your development process. If your organization doesn't invest in it then either you build it for your team or otherwise think alternate.

Another prerequisite for a successful Scrum team is the organization's culture. Think about the Scrum is building a neighborhood in the middle of a city. The culture and ecosystem of the city would heavily influence the build-up of that neighborhood. If you force-feed the alien culture into it at a certain point, it would either revolt or this would collapse. You need to change the outer system to allow it to live in harmony and prosper. So many great minds tried heart and soul to build Agile Scrum teams and either failed to reap the benefit of it or achieved mediocre success to barely deliver the minimum until collapsed. Ensure you have executive sponsorship to embrace the Agile philosophy in the outer shell I.e., the organization, otherwise think of alternate methodology.

Last but certainly not least is to have Respect in the fabric of the human behavior in the organization. This simple word has long been alienated in the professional organization with the dawn of the industrial mass production era when industry leaders had figured out that human workers can be made fungible. For Software engineering, that's not true anymore - especially when you're talking about building a new software product. If you're on the side of "everyone is fungible", you may need to choose some other software development methodologies rather than Agile.

Myth of Software Architecture in Scrum

Sometimes Agile in general and Scrum in particular is considered as the death knell for software architecture. There may be some true scurs behind that allegation however, if used pragmatically- Agile Scrum can be used without compromising the architectural rigor in software development. Here are some tips to ensure that:

- Start your first Sprint to create initial Architectural components and frameworks. The user stories and deliverables should be working software architecture with the Technical & Design documents. The key challenge is to balance how much architecture should be created upfront. The rule of thumb is to create a minimal set of architectural components that would have a high cost if changed later in the development phase. However, be ready to constantly refactor not only the code but the architecture itself.

- Constantly review the Architecture while in the Sprint, as well as before releasing the software in production.
- If you have multiple Agile Scrum teams working on the same software, then create an Architectural Review Group to periodically review the impact of the Architecturally Significant Requirements on the software architecture. Technical Leads and the Architect of the project should be part of that group.

CHAPTER VIII

Chapter 8: Software Requirement Management

Requirement Management

Requirement management is the most critical process that is prerequisite to a quality software delivery. Requirements need to be gathered, analyzed, and tracked all the way to the implementation. The poorly managed requirement not only produces poor quality software but it may also create chaos in the software project when the requirement management is loose.

Requirement Analysis

Requirement analysis is the technique to methodically analyze the software requirement and capture the right expectation of the customer. The more important but often forgotten role of requirement analysis is to define the boundary of the software and document what the software won't perform. The most crucial part of the requirement analysis is to document the requirement. The format and style of the requirement can vary but if it is not documented properly, it would wreak havoc once the software is delivered to the customer. The analysis is primarily done by Business or Systems Analysts who understand the business domain and then create requirement specification (sometime in the form of Business Requirement Document or BRD in a more traditional project and the form Use Case/User Story in a more Iterative/Agile project).

Object-Oriented Analysis

Object-Oriented Analysis is different from traditional requirement analysis. OOA outcome is primarily the Use Case where the actors and their behaviors are identified from where the software designer can easily identify the appropriate Classes, Attributes, and the Relationships among Classes. There are plenty of books and online resources available for OOA but for a quick reference visit

https://en.wikipedia.org/wiki/Object-oriented_analysis_and_design

Use Case

Use Case defines the interaction between the actor and the system to be built. This was the top tool for requirement analysis until the Agile methodologies became more prevalent. Yet, it is still the most structured way to document the requirements of the software, especially in an object-oriented software development environment. For more detail, visit *https://en.wikipedia.org/wiki/Use_case*.

User Story

User Story is the de-facto requirement gathering tool for an Agile development project. User Story defines the requirement in a prologue fashion by describing what the user wants from a system. Writing a good user story is an art and the litmus test of a good user story is the check against the INVEST criteria (*https://www.agilealliance.org/glossary/invest/*). For more detail, visit *https://www.agilealliance.org/glossary/user-stories/*

Triangulation in software requirements

I can bet that almost every software development project faces a dilemma of questioning some of the business requirements that come from the very business that you are trying to systematize. This is arguably the most dangerous zone for a software developer or a development manager to get into as your suggestion would inevitably be considered as if you are questioning their core business functional skills. But you can't just accept the requirement by its face value without doing critical analysis. After all, in the current business environment, neither the business nor the technologies independently drive the company's future. Now the sixty-four-thousand-dollar question is, how would you do it methodically? The answer lies in the word "Triangulation". This has existed in other disciplines for a long time and can be used in software development management.

Chapter 8: Software Requirement Management

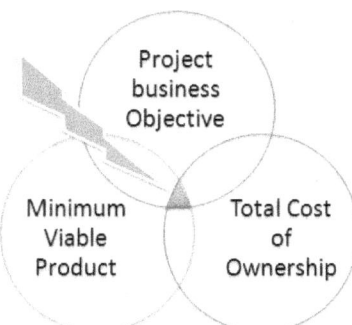

Figure-14: Triangulation in requirement management

Let's see the usage of Triangulation in another discipline. Triangulation is used by your Global Positioning System (GPS) device. There are at least three GPS Satellites that send the positions of your device that help the GPS device to accurately pinpoint your location within a few feet range.

You can use the same methodology to check if a business requirement is justified to be taken into your project as deliverables. Consider any typical business software project and you can use the following triads to justify their business requirements: (1) Project Business Objective, (2) Minimum Viable Product (MVP), and (3) Total Cost of Ownership with the perpetual cost of maintenance.

(1) Project Business Objective is the first filter you have to let the business requirement go through. If the requirement doesn't align or contradict with the project's objective, the chance is very high that there are other motivations hidden behind the requirement that needs to be unearthed

(2) Minimum Viable Product is the Lean concept where it encourages the validated learning through early delivery of the viable software with a minimum set of features. Put that requirement to the test of MVP and see if it passes or fails

(3) Total Cost of Ownership is the cost of software throughout its entire life. There's no cost-free feature in the software. Even for a feature that's working without adding a single line of code can have a high maintenance cost. There are several types of costs, such as cost of making sure that in

every subsequent upgrade you do or every new feature you add, the no-code-feature has to be tested to make sure that it functions as is; if you find a better technology/algorithm to implement in that software which would stop that no-code-feature to function, then you either have to stick to the inferior technology/algorithm or now add code to make that no-code-feature to work.

Finally, never forget to identify the true need of the business (sometimes referred to as "problem statement") behind that requirement. You would often find that the true need may be vastly different than the very requirement is trying to solve and the requirement may be a solution that the business person came up with to solve that true need. Knowing the true business need would allow you to come up with a true solution to that problem which may be much simpler to implement. Undoubtedly, the simplest solution is the best solution and you would need a complex thought process to come up with that simplest solution. ⚠

Software Cost Estimation

Software Estimation is often considered as wizardry which is mostly neglected during the inception of an Information Technology Project, nonetheless almost always is used to formulate two most important attributes of a project i.e., the cost and the deadline, and often with a rigid expectation of a high level of accuracy to hit the targeted project deadline.

There is a vicious cycle in the whole estimation thing: when executives ask the Project Manager for estimation, it is often portrayed as, which should always be the true purpose of estimation, that is, to get a "ballpark" figure to gauge the depth of the water or to be specific, should the executive be bothered about the project and invest her time to materialize the project from its conception. But, as soon as the estimation is handed over for that project, that number is considered as a commitment from the project manager. Later on, if that project deviates from that supposedly "ballpark figure" estimation, the project manager is personally held liable for that deviation.

Chapter 8: Software Requirement Management

So, the project managers are either unwilling to provide an estimation at all or pad the estimation to cover themselves from the uncertainties and unknowns of projects. This is a classic "catch 22" situation for most of the project managers who are managing software development projects or planning to start a career as Project Manager of Information Technology. Now, the million-dollar question would be: how a Project Manager should walk over that double edge sword, if you will, to provide the true estimation of a software project without falling into that "commitment" trap.

I answer that question including an overview of some of the well-known, in terms of market share and most commonly used software cost-estimation models such as Function Point Analysis, Use Case Point, and Heuristic method. I am going to provide a framework and guideline to help the Software Team Leaders and Software Project Managers to choose the right estimation model for their software projects. In the following section, I am providing a list of best practices to fight the "estimation fatigue" and prepare them to duck the most common pitfalls where they're forced to respond with a "ballpark figure" in a very early stage of projects, sometime during a water-cooler conversation. There is an important but often ignored characteristic of the software estimation which is called "the cone of uncertainty". I will also touch upon that characteristic in brief by showing how to effectively use that phenomenon

Chapter 8: Software Requirement Management

to build confidence and earn the trust of the executive sponsors and senior management of the organization.

The cone of uncertainty

Before learning any techniques of cost estimation, let's understand the nature of uncertainty involved in estimating software projects. A software project is all about unknowns. At the beginning of a software project, the project charter takes a very simplistic view of the final product and tries to estimate the dollar amount (because as we learned, the project sponsor always looks at the bottom line which is the dollar cost of the project). At this stage, the larger amounts of unknown create a larger uncertainty in estimation. But as the project moves into the deeper level of planning and implementation, the more unknown becomes known, hence the uncertainty in the estimation becomes lesser compared to the previous stage. This phenomenon is described by the concept of "The Cone of Uncertainty", originally used in the chemical industry by the founders of the American Association of Cost Engineers (now AACE International) and got wide popularity after it is published in Steve McConnell's famous book "Software Estimation: Demystifying the Black Art".

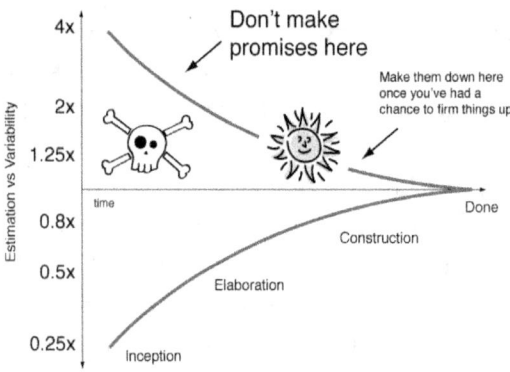

Figure-15: The Cone of Uncertainty from www.agilenutshell.com

According to the above graph, it is evident that the later in the project life cycle, the better the estimation. But the 'catch 22' of this reality is, no one would come to the one-stage down towards the certainty if the initial

154

Chapter 8: Software Requirement Management

estimation (which is bound to be inaccurate due to the high error margin) is not given at the project inception.

So, can this cone be beaten? As Steve McConnell mentioned – "Consider the effect of the Cone of Uncertainty on the accuracy of your estimate. Your estimate cannot have more accuracy than is possible at your project's current position within the Cone. Another important – and difficult – concept is that the Cone of Uncertainty represents the best-case accuracy that is possible to have in software estimates at different points in a project. The Cone represents the error in estimates created by skilled estimators. It is easily possible to do worse. It isn't possible to be more accurate; it's only possible to be luckier" ⚠. Now the only option left is to live with the cone of uncertainty. Below are a few techniques on how to deal with that reality:

- Be honest and upfront about the reality. Though it may not be taken as a positive gesture initially, being truthful about the risk of estimating with the expectation of high accuracy would pay off in the long run. If the project sponsors can be convinced with the reality of software projects (probably by showing some of the past histories of software projects within that organization), maybe padding onto the final numbers may give everyone sufficient wiggle room.
- Attach the variability with the estimation when presenting to the project sponsors. There's no benefit to anyone in that project to surprise the stakeholders.
- Actively work on resolving the uncertainty by making the unknowns known. This is the responsibility of the estimation team to force the cone of uncertainty to narrow down. Without active and conscious actions, narrowing down the cone won't happen won't happen on its own with the progression of the project's life cycle.

Let's try to take a postmortem look at why we have this cone of uncertainty in our software projects. The single most reason for the uncertainty of the estimation is that the estimation is doing a prediction (or forecast) on the capabilities of software developers. Unfortunately, by nature, human behavior is unpredictable. The same person can behave differently based on the presence or absence of surrounding factors. A programmer may come up with the solution of a complex programming problem in a few minutes whereas the same programmer may struggle to resolve a lesser complex problem in another time. So, the entire game of prediction is bound to fall apart when it is trying to predict the most unpredictable nature of human psychology. So, the strategy shouldn't be to try to hit the bull's eye with a single estimation value, rather try to maximize the chance of coming close to the actual with the estimation through the use of techniques like range value, plus-minus factor, confidence level, etc. If you fail to effectively estimate the software delivery, you may end up giving an estimation that couldn't be kept as promised. Hence, it will be labeled as the project that has failed, whereas it was your estimation that was incorrect in the very first place. That's why sometimes it is said that we don't have failed projects but just failed estimations.

Though we're living with this cone of uncertainty in every software project, we remain oblivious to reality and pretend that didn't exist. Anyway, I hope we won't be from now on.

Standard estimation models and methods

Let's first start with the basics of estimation and then I will touch upon some of the popular and useful estimation models. This will give a solid foundation for the upcoming sections of Software Cost Estimation.

A Google search reveals the meaning of estimation as "a rough calculation of the value, number, quantity, or extent of something". By definition, "estimation" is a rough calculation. But when people in software development hear the word "estimation" they internally treat it as "actual". Software Estimation is often seen as wizardry which is mostly neglected during the inception of an Information Technology Project. Nonetheless, almost always is used to formulate the two most important attributes of a project i.e., the cost and the deadline, and often with a rigid expectation of a high level of accuracy.

Software Estimation is widely, and in some cases, an overused topic in the field of computer science and software engineering. People were looking for a panacea where one can predict the schedule. A wide range of models has been developed since the twentieth century to solve the premise of sizing the software before it is built. Some of them are very effective at their time with a certain programming practice whereas the usefulness of some of them transcended the boundary of technology and programming practices. Here are some of the very popular and widely used software cost estimation models and metrics.

Line of Code (LOC/SLOC)

Though Line of Code (LOC) or Source Line of Code (SLOC) is not a software estimation model in itself, this is the most widely used metric in software estimation models to determine the size e.g., COCOMO, SLIM, SEER-SEM, PRICE-S. Moreover, the majority of the ad-hoc estimation models used in the software house, use this metric as an input to estimate the software development effort. The popularity of the LOC is not because this gives an accurate picture of the size of the software but due to its simplistic connotation to the direct result of programming work of developing a software product. The primary advantage of SLOC is that it is easily agreeable by the parties that are involved in the project to consider SLOC for software sizing as the source code is the apparent building block of the software. Despite its sheer popularity, the use of LOC in software estimation is the biggest contributor to estimation in-accuracy. The reasons behind this inaccuracy are:

- There's no standard or single agreed-upon method on counting Source Line of Code (SLOC) in a language-dependent way; changing the programming language immediately impacts the count of it.
- It is inherently inconceivable to predict SLOC from a scope document with a very high level of requirements.
- There's a psychological toll of SLOC as it may incentivize the bad coding practice thus increasing the SLOC.

COCOMO

COCOMO stands for **CO**nstructive **CO**st **MO**del, is one of the early generation software cost estimation models, and enjoyed its early popularity in the nineteen-eighties. It uses Line of Code as a basis of estimation and suffers all the shortcomings that I mentioned above in SLOC. I believe COCOMO is not very effective in this software development age where Object-Oriented Programming rules the world and LOC doesn't make a whole lot of sense in OOP in terms of effort estimation. Learn more from *http://en.wikipedia.org/wiki/COCOMO* and *http://www.softstarsystems.com/overview.htm*.

Function Point Analysis

The obvious limitations on guessing LOC of a to-be-built software paved the way for another popular and somewhat realistic solution during the early phase of a software project, which is called Function Point Analysis (FPA). In FPA, the software size is measured through a construct called 'Function Points' (FP). Function points allow the measurement of software size in standard units, independent of the underlying language in which the software is developed. Instead of counting the lines of code that make up a system, count the number of externals (inputs, outputs, inquiries, and interfaces) that make up the system.

There are five types of externals to count: External inputs, External outputs, External inquiries, External interfaces, and Internal data files. The below Value Adjustment Multiplier (VAM) formula is used to obtain the function point count:

$$\text{VAM} = \sum_{i=1}^{14} V_i * 0.01 + 0.65$$

Where Vi is a rating of 0 to 5 for fourteen predefined factors.

The primary advantage of using the Function Point Analysis model is that it measures the size of the solution rather than the problem and is extremely useful for the transaction processing systems (e.g., MIS applications). Moreover, FPA can be derived directly from the requirements and easily understood by the non-technical user. However, it does not provide an accurate estimate when dealing with command-

and-control software, switching software, systems software, or embedded systems. Moreover, FPA isn't very effective in Object-Oriented software development that uses Use Cases and converting Use Cases into Function Points may be counter-intuitive.

Use Case Points Method (UUCPM)

Similar in concept to function points, the theoretical basis of the Use Case Points Method, first described by Gustav Karner, is based on use cases as a basic notation for the representation of functionality, and uses case points, like function points, measure the size of the system. Once we know the approximate size of a system, we can derive an expected duration for the project if we also know (or can estimate) the team's rate of progress. In this approach, the first step is to calculate a measure called the Unadjusted Use Case Point (UUCP) count. The UUCP count applies a technical adjustment factor, just like FPA, albeit the factors themselves have been changed to reflect the different methodology that underpins development with a use case. The UUCPM also defines a set of environmental (project) factors that contribute to a weighting factor that is also used to modify the UUCP measure. Four important formulas used in UCP is Unadjusted Use case Points (UUCP), Technical Complexity Factor (TCF), Environment Factor (EF) and Use Case Point (UCP):

$$1. UUCP = \sum_{i=1}^{6} n_i * w_i$$

Where n_i is the Actor or Use Case, and w_i is the Weighting

$$2. TCF = C_1 + C_2 \sum_{i=1}^{13} F_i * W_i \qquad \text{Where } C_1 = 0.6 \text{ and } C_2 = 0.01$$

$$2. EF = C_1 + C_2 \sum_{i=1}^{8} F_i * W_i \qquad \text{Where } C_1 = 1.4 \text{ and } C_2 = 0.03$$

$$3. UCP = UUCP * TCF * EF$$

Once the number of the UCP has been determined, an effort estimate can be calculated by multiplying the number of UCP by a fixed number of hours.

The primary advantage of the UCP model is that it can be automated thus saving the team a great deal of estimating time. Of course, there's the counter-argument that an estimate is only as good as the effort put into it. Additionally, they are a very pure measure of size as it allows separating estimating size from deriving duration. Moreover, by establishing average implementation time per UCP, forecasting is possible for future schedules. On the contrary, the fundamental problem with UCP is that the estimate cannot be arrived at until all of the use cases are written. While use case points may work well for creating a rough, initial estimate of overall project size, they are much less useful in driving the iteration-to-iteration work of a team. A related issue is that the rules for determining, for instance, what constitutes a transaction are imprecise and since the detail in a use case varies tremendously by the author of the use case, the approach is flawed. Moreover, few Technical Factors do not have an impact across the overall project; the way they are multiplied by the weight does impact the overall size. The installation ease factor is an example of such. Finally, like most other estimation models, they do not fit into the agile development methodology.

User Story Points (USP)

User stories, which help to shift the focus from writing about requirements to talking about them, are the foundational block of the Agile development technique. All Agile user stories include a written sentence or two, and more importantly a series of conversations about the desired functionality from the perspective of the user of the system. In the Agile world, the method of estimating the size of the software is the User Story Points which is the unit of measure for expressing the overall size of a user story, feature, or other pieces of work. It tells us how big a story is, relative to others, either in terms of size or complexity by using relative sizing the technique. Popular sizing techniques include- Fibonacci series (1, 2, 3, 5, 8, 13, 21, etc.) and T-shirt size (S, M, L, XL, XXL, etc.). It is recommended to estimate the size of each user story with the entire team, usually through planning poker sessions.

The major advantage of User Story Point is that it is relatively easy and fun to estimate the relative size of a user story. Also, the estimated size of the product is the outcome of a consensus of the team, so the ownership lies to the team, which has a psychological influence to achieve higher throughput. On the contrary, benchmarking of size is challenging as the story points taken by one team cannot be compared with another team's USP. Also, some people may find it hard to get to the duration form the USP as there's practically no direct relationship between user story point and person hour. If the team is not diverse enough to balance out the skewed sizing due to the biases of a particular group, the sizing, eventually, could be proved to be useless. A subtle risk exists of inflated sizing by the development team if management has unrealistic expectations to show higher velocity to prove productivity.

Delphi Method

The Delphi Method is an information-gathering technique that was created in the 1950s by the RAND Corporation. The Delphi Method is based on the surveys and makes use of the information of the participants, who mainly are experts in their area. Under this method of software, project specifications would be given to a few experts and their opinion is taken. The steps taken to get the estimation using are (i) Selection of experts, (ii) Briefing the experts about the project, objective of the estimation and overall project scope and clarification, (iii) Collate the estimates (software size and development effort) received from the experts and finally (iv) Convergence of estimates and finalization.

The major advantages of the Delphi technique are that it is very simple to administer and also can be derived relatively quicker. Also, it doesn't need any in-house expertise within the organization and can hire external experts with the domain knowledge to come out with a quick estimate. On the contrary, the disadvantages primarily come from selecting the wrong experts as well as getting an adequate number of experts willing to participate in the estimation. Moreover, it is not possible to determine the causes of variance between the estimated value and the actual values.

Heuristic Method

Heuristic methods of estimation are essentially based on the experience that exists within a particular organization where past projects are used to estimate the required resources necessary to deliver future projects. A convenient sub-classification is to divide heuristic methods into 'top-down' and 'bottom-up' approaches. These approaches are the de-facto methods by which estimates are produced and as such, they are implicated in being poor reflections of the actual resources that are required as evidenced by the failure of projects to be estimated accurately. Top-down approaches to effort estimation may rely on the opinion of an expert whereas the Bottom-up estimation is the process by which time needed to code each identified module is estimated based on the discrete tasks that must be performed, such as analysis, design and project management.

Despite its simplistic approach, the error margin of heuristic method estimation is not proven to be worse than any other parametric or algorithmic (COCOMO, UUCP, etc.) estimation models. This doesn't come free of risk either. The lack of access to historical data will cause a high degree of error margin of future projects and the underlying assumption of repeatability of organizations' success could be proved to be deadly. Moreover, if not conducted systematically, tasks such as integration, quality, and configuration could be overlooked

There is another category that usually people don't talk about a lot, which is - a homegrown estimation model. Those models are created by the team members of a software project where they're working for quite a long period and those work pretty well for their projects. As those kinds of estimation models typically aren't standardized to use for software projects outside of that group, those are usually not made public.

Chapter 8: Software Requirement Management

Choose the right Estimation Model

The availability of a vast number of software estimation models sometimes makes it confusing for the project manager and for the technical team to choose the right estimation model. Moreover, not everyone wants to be an expert in estimation techniques and models. If you have enough budget allocated for the planning phase of your project (I doubt you would often get that in any software project), you can hire an estimation expert who would have detailed expertise on various software cost estimation models and choose the right model for your project. But for those who don't want to invest their time to go through all the estimation models (some of which I already have explained briefly), I've created a sample matrix that would provide some sort of guideline to help you identify the right estimation model. At the very least, it would give you a starting point.

	Procedural Programming	Object Oriented Programing	Availability of past project information	Business users Participation	Availability of industry Experts	Availability of internal experts	Agile Method	Iterative Method
COCOMO	✓	✓						✓
Function Point Analysis	✓							✓
Use Case Point		✓					~	~
User Story Point		✓		✓		✓	✓	~
Heuristic Method	✓	✓	✓			✓		✓
Expert Judgment	✓	✓	~		✓	~	✓	✓
Delphi Method	✓	✓		✓	✓	~	✓	✓
Estimation by Analogy	✓	✓	✓			✓	✓	✓
SLIM	✓	✓	✓					✓

Legend

✓ Fits well   ~ May fit after tweaking the model   BLANK SPACE   Neutral

Figure-16: Estimation techniques and applicability in SDLC

For example, if the software project uses the Object-Oriented Programming technology, almost all the estimation models can be used. Now if the development methodology is taken into consideration and if it happens to use Agile Development methodology, then the options become narrow. In that case, a few of the above models remain to be a pick from the matrix e.g., Use Case Point, User Story Point, and Delphi Method. Though the above framework would provide some initial guidelines to narrow down the list of models, in the end, it is up to the Project Manager and the Software development team to decide on the best fit models for their project.

If I were you, I would not settle on a single estimation model from the above matrix but try out at least two to three estimation methods for my initial estimation and if all of them comes with the proximity of 10% - 20%, then probably you can go with any of those you like. But if you find a large gap in your initial estimations from those different methods, then you better be very careful while providing your commitment to the company executives. The variation in estimations tells you that you're handling a project that has more unknowns and a lot of uncertainties. I believe we haven't forgotten the lesson of the cone of uncertainty.

Software estimation best practices

Finally, we're at the point where we now know why we develop estimation fatigue when asked to estimate a software project and also we've visited some of the options that we have to avoid that fatigue. But If all of those seem too much for you, and if you have a project in hand, and can't wait to read through all those sections then you can just go over this section and use it as a jump starter for your project. The best practices described here can be used with the use of any specific standard software estimation model or no model at all:

- Estimate the effort in terms of scenarios i.e., Best Case and Worst-Case scenario and then take the average of both to set the target date of your project.[21]

Chapter 8: Software Requirement Management

- Create the estimations in the form of range value rather than a single number estimation. After all, the estimation is an educated guess, so you don't need to pretend that you have the psychic power to reveal a golden number. ⚠
- When the project has lots of uncertainties and unknowns, provide multiple estimations with a different set of assumptions associated with those.
- Use a confidence-based estimation when you're hard-pressed to give a single estimation point. E.g., If you're given no chance but told to deliver the software before the Christmas day, then the estimation could be given as – Release date on Christmas day (with confidence level 60%).
- The ballpark figure is a dangerous trap, never fall into that. If you're forced to give ballpark figure estimation, never forget to add the underlying assumptions and associated risks along with that estimation.
- Trust your intuition, never fear to use Estimation by Analogy technique. Though Estimation by Analogy may seem dangerous, if the organization takes similar projects repeatedly, be bold to take that route. This is not less accurate than other standard estimation methods, nevertheless the quickest and cheapest of all.
- Empirical estimation models need time to be matured and predictable. If the software project is a one-time endeavor and may not be repeated, do not use the empirical estimation model. The promise of improving the accuracy can't be harvested without repetition.
- Estimation should be done at the most possible granular level (also known as Bottom-up Estimation) and then roll up to the complete project level to get the project estimation. The granular level estimation offsets most of the inaccuracies in estimation.
- Estimation at granular levels can be used to defend your estimation as well. Management tends to raise the question to a lump sum estimation of a project but would think twice to question a granular level of each feature that aggregate into the project level estimation. Moreover, when you will be asked to add a new feature in the software (and it is almost

guaranteed that you would be asked for it), that granularity would help you to identify features that you can trade-in, otherwise you would have no choice but to swallow the "asks" into your project.
- If you choose to use a standard software estimation model, use at least two models and compare the results. If they come close then it would give you more confidence in your estimation.
- Revisit the estimation once the project is completed. This time, re-estimate the relative size of each task as well as the actual effort hours and record them. Once you have enough empirical data, you can use them in your future projects to provide a ballpark figure when asked by executive management.
- It is as important to communicate the estimation right as the estimation process itself. Oftentimes a great deal of time and money is invested in the estimation process whereas leaving the presentation of the estimation unfocused. It is also very important to set the right tone that creates an environment of acceptance. I've compiled some of the communication best practices for software estimation that, if followed appropriately, can increase the chance of acceptance of your estimation:
- Don't fall into the trap of telling what the project sponsors and executives want to hear. Because you are the one who would be held responsible for the estimation commitment that you are making.
- Document all the assumptions that were made throughout the estimation process. For example, if the estimation value is converted into time duration, make sure to document what was the competency level of programmers that were assumed to get the person day.
- Educate your stakeholders about the "cone of uncertainty" of the software estimation process. The stakeholders will be more susceptible to accept the higher error margin when the estimation is made early in the project's life cycle, as shown in the "cone of uncertainty".
- Always present the estimation in terms of a range value rather than one single number. By definition, the word estimation is a rough calculation. So, it wouldn't be a wise idea to present the estimation as a single number which would mislead the audience about its perceived accuracy.

Chapter 8: Software Requirement Management

- If necessary to provide a single value estimation, use the plus-or-minus qualifier e.g., rather than saying that the software would take 6 months, express it in 6 months +- 2 months. So, the stakeholders get what they wanted, and the estimator is protected from a future ungrounded accusation.
- You can also use a confidence factor while presenting your estimation. As an example, it is better to communicate that you are, for instance, 70% confident that the project would be completed in 6 months i.e. if the project is targeted to deliver at the end of 6 months, there's a 30% chance of missing the deadline.
- Don't pretend the all-sunny day scenario for your project. Though some people may consider it as a pessimistic approach, communicating the predicted implementation risks. Add the perceived risks that were identified during the estimation process and use them to come up with a plus-minus qualifier, range, and confidence level based single estimation.
- Even though it may not be asked, it is better to present more than one estimation value with a different set of scopes. As for an example: if you have a system to develop that has 100 use cases, you may provide two estimations: one for the entire set i.e., 100 use cases and another is for top 80% use cases. It would help you to avoid the trap of "everything is required" statement. In reality that's always not true. So, if the estimation of everything seems too long to the stakeholders, there's an alternative with a reduced set of features, analogous to the options offered by your GPS navigation tool when you are driving - shortest distance or shortest time; and you do the picking.

There's a wise saying that "we don't fail a project but we fail to estimate it right". I hope now you would have a better way of estimating your software projects thus achieving a higher rate of success.

CHAPTER IX

Chapter 9: Software Quality Management

Chapter 9: Software Quality Management

Many times, a development manager may or may not manage both developers and Test Engineers. However, if you're managing them both, then this is for you. Nonetheless, you would be interacting with the SQA manager or SQA leads, so knowing the SQA process brings an edge to your management skill. Due to the focus of the book, I would touch only briefly about the philosophy of Software Quality Assurance (SQA) instead of going into the details of the discipline itself. This is not because the SQA is any less important than the development but because of that, the SQA needs a complete book to cover its tools and processes. To start with, here's a short note on SQA as a process:

SQA team uses Test Strategy, Test Plan, Test Case, and Test Scenarios as primary artifacts. In a software project, there should be at least one Test Strategy, one or more Test Plans, scores of Test Cases, and their corresponding Test Scenarios.

SQA Process

SQA is the process to ensure that the software is certified based on the company set policy and doesn't go out of the door without that certification. As a principle, I always treated SQA as my ally because I, as a developer, was the most beneficiary of that process. The SQA should be empowered to that point where they should be at a level where nothing can go around that. In the SQA team, the engineers do both automated and manual testing. Test automation should complement the developer's unit test suite. Combining both developers' unit test suite and SQA automated test suite, the software would be easy to refactor and regress tests. This would make sure the team can change the software in the shortest period. One thing to keep in mind is that automated test coverage shouldn't be treated as the silver bullet. The primary reason is the cost of maintaining 100% automated code coverage but this automated test would leave some of the tricky but deadliest bugs to sip through.

Create Test Strategy

The QA process starts with the creation of a Test Strategy. This artifact is created to document what kind of plans would be used to test specific areas of the software e.g., Database Testing, Web UI testing, Business Logic testing, Server-side testing, etc. Usually, the QA lead or QA manager creates this artifact. As a best practice, review the Test Strategy with the stakeholders, such as Development Lead, Analyst Lead, and Architect to make sure to capture their inputs and suggestions.

Create Test Plan

Sometimes Test Strategy covers the plan however, for a large and long running software project, a separate Test Plan is created to capture the detail plan for each release, components, and subsystems The Test Plan covers the detail of how the test would be conducted for each area in the Test Strategy. For example, what would be done to test the web application interface, external integration or Database?

Create Test Case and Test Scenario

The Test Case and Test Scenarios are individual testing with input values and the expected outcome of it. For example, a test case is taking a particular piece of functionality and defines the input data set and then derives the expected output values for that particular functionality.

Create Test Environment

Test environment creation should be automated so that QA team members can easily create a new environment for a clean test setup. Nowadays, the use of Containerized (usually Docker) environments makes it very easy to do that. If not, use automation and scripts to create/clean up the Test environment.

Test Data Management

Test data can be as simple as few inputs and expected output data. However, depending on your project your test data management can itself be a discipline itself. Usually, the test data creation is managed through a script that can create the test data and clean up after testing is done. It may include creating a test environment if the software needs a dedicated test setup.

Execute Test

The core activity of QA is to execute the Test Cases and find bugs in the software. Use of Test Management tools like Bugzilla or Atlassian Jira should be absolutely must. The workflow within that tool should be used to manage the test process.

Communicate Test Result

Usually, the QA team schedules regular Triage meetings to review the identified bugs with developers. The QA team should be very crispy and meticulous about communication. Few of the key aspects are:

- Each Test Case execution outcome should be coupled with a clear test evidence and a write-up on "how to reproduce", preferably visually with screenshots or videos. This is very critical for two reasons (a) this alleviates the back-and-forth between Developer and QA member whether this is really a bug or not and (b) it helps a developer tremendously to quickly figure out the bug and fix it. Otherwise, you will end up a frustrated developer who will always push back on fixing the bugs. ⚠
- Bugs are recorded with priority and severity for appropriate responses. Sample severities are: Critical, Major, Moderate, Minor, and Cosmetic. Sample priorities are: High, Medium, Low or P1, P2, P3.
- Come to the Triage meeting prepared to answer any question from the developers. This is also a good place to come to agreement on the Priority and Severity as many times, Developer and QA members have conflict of interest in the bugs. So, use this forum to smooth it out.
- Create metrics and statistics of Testing progress. Few of the important metrics are: percentage of Test Case completion, Bug vs. Requirement ratio, Bug reopen count, Histogram of Bugs in terms of severity and priority, top bug resolver and top bug contributor (use it wisely), etc.

How much testing is enough for software?

This is a million-dollar question, especially when you're in a release crunch time and you are in a project where you don't have automated test suites for your, technically speaking, "System Under Test" (SUT). So, how would you define the testing boundary of software? Like most other questions in this world, the answer is: it depends. It depends on what you would test, why you would test, and most importantly how would you test it- manually or in an automated fashion. For the remainder of this section let me clarify what I consider as the goal of software testing – the goal of software testing is to certify the behaviors of software by documenting the result. Releasing software to the end-user is a whole different ball game and SQA is one of the key players among several other key players.

Let's first take the most important factor i.e., how you're testing. If you happen to have the fully automated test cases and test suits, my immediate response would be - Run'em all. This is the safest and most cost-efficient way to certify the behavior of the software. Like Microsoft way, for MS Windows they execute the entire test suite and build it every night. If you can afford it then do it, why take the chance. In the statistical world, we take a sample because getting the entire population of data is unrealistic. Similarly, if you don't have that luxury then you pick and choose based on the reality and expectations set for the software. I've explained it later in this chapter.

Now the next factor is when you're testing with the assumption that you don't have automated test coverage (or at least the time frame doesn't allow you to develop the fully automated test suites) and you have to test the software manually to certify it. If you are under pressure to complete the testing within a specified time frame then my suggestion would be to go for a targeted test. To determine what and how much to test, follow the Goldilocks principle - don't over test it nor under test it, but the test which is JUST RIGHT. You'll always find that you can cover 80% of the software's feature by executing just around 20% of the test cases that you have and you would spend the remaining 80% of your resources to cover the rest;

check the famous 80-20 rule to learn about it from *http://en.wikipedia.org/wiki/Pareto_principle*. To identify that 20%, test cases and run them and if you're asked to release your software before you can open the remaining test cases, go ahead and release the software. One important thing to remember, make sure you release it with a confidence factor attached with it - for instance when you run 80% test cases of it, label it as "QA certified with 80% confidence". I know you can't release it to the external world with that tag but you should have that number tagged with it to communicate the risk factor to the management. This is very important to document for future improvement.

The last but not the least factor is- what are you testing. If you're testing NASA's space flight module, you have no choice but to test it fully and, in that case, you're certainly not told to test it by a certain time frame, and the release date of the software (i.e., the mission launch date) would be determined by when you're able to complete 100% of the testing. The same is true when you're talking about medical equipment software or life support systems. But when you're testing non-mission-critical systems and missing a bug in the software won't take the company down (I remember once I logged into Facebook and I was taken to profile of someone else while I could see a certain photo album of mine within that profile; which happened in around 2010 and now in 2018, Facebook turned out as the de-facto platform for social networking - that bug was surely missed out by some test engineer but who did care about that) and you're given a deadline to meet, go ahead boldly with confidence based testing. One more thing about test coverage: there are some situations where you want to test both positive and negative test cases for a feature and in other situations where you're just fine to run only positive test cases (this is applicable for the software that is built to use in-house and won't ever go out of the corporate intranet boundary)

The bottom line is, you always want to create every possible test case for every feature and run them all but you need to act based on the reality on the ground and don't hesitate to take calculated risks.

Alternative strategies of Software Testing

Nobody denies the fact that software should be tested and the best way to ensure that is by testing every feature of it. That's a no-brainer, and to understand that we don't need to be an expert in QA or software development. But, often, the reality on the ground may not allow the QA team to go through that "best" route to make the software "bug-free". So, what are the alternatives that we have to release software with an optimal level of testing when reality doesn't let you execute the complete test suite? I have broadly touched on that in the "how much testing is enough for software?" with few tips on how to justify the QA test strategy to perform partial testing. Let's take a look into it from a different perspective to derive some kind of strategy that would allow the QA team to react during the time of necessity.

There could be several scenarios that would demand to react differently. However, I would like to focus on three test strategies that I found helpful based on my experience and also probably cover much of the testing ground.

Risk-Weighted Testing

This testing strategy takes back to the basic question on why in the first place we need a QA team and what's the purpose of testing. To me, the QA process exists in the Systems Development Life Cycle (SDLC) to reduce the risk of slipping bugs into the production environment i.e., to the end-users. I know this would immediately stir up controversy but there's a reason why I am saying that. You ask the question to any software professional (including QA professional) if they dare to proclaim the tested software as "completely" bug-free after the QA release. I can guarantee you that nobody would dare to claim. The reason is, the QA process makes software relatively bug free and makes it usable to an extent that is proportionate to the price paid by the end-users. Having said all of that, the best strategy, at the time of release deadline and cost crunch, to effectively conduct the testing would be going with the Risk-Weighted Testing (RWT) approach. In this strategy, the risk associated with each functionality would be calculated in several dimensions and rank them to create an ordered list. That ranked list would be used in a pragmatic fashion depending on the budget, time, and resource constraints. If the time is the constraint and only a few days are given to the QA team, then the QA team should start from the top-ranked functionality and go through the list sequentially. On the other hand, if the QA team is asked to take as minimum functionalities as possible to test, they should draw a line where it would cover the most risk with the least resource (*http://en.wikipedia.org/wiki/Pareto_principle*).

The primary challenge of this strategy is to create the risk-weighted list of functionalities. Several techniques and tools that can be used and here I'm explaining a few of them:

- *Brainstorming*: the most efficient and cost-effective method is to have software developers, business analysts, testers, and end-users in a conference room and brainstorm the list. People often misuse the term Brainstorming (http://en.wikipedia.org/wiki/Brainstorming) by just having a controlled discussion but if brainstorming is done properly, it can create a dramatic positive result.
- *Delphi method*: if you have access to a group of experts, you can use the Delphi method (http://en.wikipedia.org/wiki/Delphi_method) where the experts can take all the functionality of the software and risk-weight them through a rigorous round of refinement. This is comparatively costlier than Brainstorming.
- *Analogy technique*: using the past experience within the same company, the potential risks of functionality can be identified. This is the least expensive but often most effective if there are a high number of reference projects available with expert personnel to make that analogy.
- There also exist *Quantitative Approaches* like Monte-Carlo simulation, PERT distributions, etc. to use to create the risk ranked list if appropriate resources are available.

Change Oriented Testing

In one of my projects, we had introduced a bug into a perfectly working functionality while implementing an enhancement by modifying a common piece of code. An unrelated functionality, though it had been proven to not be so unrelated, got broken due to that change in the common code which was done for the right purpose i.e., to achieve code reusability and with the right intention. Unfortunately, the bug introduced due to that enhancement slipped through to production. This provoked me to think about the existing testing strategy which proved to be insufficient to provide good solid test coverage (and everyone takes their best shot to squeeze QA cycle as much as they could do). To avoid that kind of situation, this Change Oriented Test (COT) strategy where the Development team and QA team would work hand in hand to identify what piece of code or component is changed in the software with the potential impact areas (often labeled as functionality). The basic and foundation could be a simple Change-Functionality Impact Matrix that would capture changes as rows and functionalities as columns with X-marked intersection as impact. The QA team can't develop this matrix alone by themselves but with the help of the Development team, a fairly accurate matrix can be created where it would be possible to identify the impact areas and then subsequently plan for the testing to cover the impacted functionalities.

To make it successful, the below steps should be continued to be in place in the SDLC:

- In every release, the Development team will create a mapping of code components to requirements and hand it over to the QA team ahead of the testing cycle.
- The release note would have one section explaining the changes along with the published impact matrix.

The downside of this strategy is that if an automated tool (and embedded in IDE) isn't used, it would be very expensive to manually manage and keep the impact matrix up to date.

Usage-Driven Testing

This approach of testing computer software or systems isn't something that is novel but what I found is that this isn't used explicitly in the Software Development Life Cycle (SDLC) by the Quality Assurance (QA) team. At least I haven't seen that in any Test Strategy document or Test Plan where the QA team has a concrete plan on studying and analyzing end users' behavior and psychology to come up with the Usage-Driven test plan, test scenario, and test data.

The fundamental idea behind this strategy is to focus on the features or areas that the users would use most. The automatic next question would be - "how would you know before you release the software?" Yes, I don't have a crystal ball to forecast that but it may not be impossible to get an idea of it, though.

- Surveying among the business users on their priority ranking of every feature of the software. Then draw a line at, for the sake of the discussion, the third quartile and test all the features thoroughly that fall within that bucket while leaving the rest to smoke only.
- Another approach could be shadowing users' day to day activity to come up with the list of most usage. The limitation of that is you can only do that if you're automating existing business processes, enhancing existing software, or rebuilding software, etc.
- The last and the least preferred with the highest risk option could be to use expert judgment and pick your list. This approach is better than to release software by random testing or half-done testing with no strategy.

I would like to reiterate this at the conclusion that all of the above testing strategies should be considered only in a situation where the full testing cycle cannot be performed and the senior management understands and makes the conscious call to go with those alternate routes to meet the business need e.g., customer need, time to market, beat the competitors, etc.

Debugging is more of an art than science

As a professional software developer or a manager of software developers, one thing is sure that you would have to live with the reality of software with bugs. Knowing the principle would be crucial for you to help improve your team's ability to investigate software bugs more efficiently. Though there's no set procedure on how to debug a software code, I suggest to use the below guiding principles:

- The first principle is – the more complex and impactful the software bug is, the sillier the root cause would be. So never ignore to test the simplest part of it. E.g., have you used the same Java version consistently across the environments? Once I had to resolve a bug where the JVM was using Solaris version and I was testing it on Windows JVM and the Solaris JVM wasn't considering the Daylight Savings Time (DST) thus giving me one day less for a particular date range.
- If the application that was working smoothly and now started to error out then look for what has changed since last time it worked properly. In the majority of the cases, the code or infrastructure that has changed holds the root cause of the bug.
- When changing code to debug the software, don't change more than one area at a time even if you are tempted to do so to quickly resolve the issue. Patience is the true virtue of debugging. This is one of the reasons why a whole lot of professionals do not want to be a software engineer.
- In some cases, where the application bug is performance-related, rather than looking for the silver bullet and waiting to improve the performance of the entire application, minimize or localize the issue to a subset of application's functionalities so that you can buy some time to resolve it application-wide. I had once faced an application bug where the entire application was infrequently getting frozen – once or twice in a month (later on I found that it was an Oracle RAC's bug with distributed two-phase commit transaction that keeps the lock of a table and doesn't sync that lock information with the other RAC instance). I had changed the code to localize that application-wide freezing down to a single user-level locking until I had the root cause identified and resolved for good.
- When you are using various software technologies and vendors, you would surely be played like a ping-pong ball by the vendors. For the above bug in the Oracle RAC configuration, we had DBAs blaming Java developers for the application locking, Oracle vendor was blaming IBM

Chapter 9: Software Quality Management

to lock the transaction on the WebSphere application server, IBM was blaming the Oracle JDBC driver to retain the lock instead of releasing the lock after a set timeout. At once, they had even blamed the underlying Network connection by suggesting that the TCP packet was being dropped by the network switch.

OpenAI, an AI research and deployment company, has released chatGPT (*https://chat.openai.com/chat*) in November that seems to completely change how do you even approach a code or debug a piece of code. It brings enormous power to developers. The way we can clearly distinguish a developer's life before and after Google came to the world, chatGPT is probably another distinctive moment where a developer's life is going to be completely redefined from now on. If you haven't tried it, I would strongly suggest you to try today. The possibilities are almost limitless however, you can try below to start with:

- Ask chatGPT for snippet of code.
- Copy the piece of code that's giving you error and ask why it's not working. You will be astonished.

```
why this isn't working public class Main {
    public static void main(String[] args) {
        String url = "jdbc:postgresql://localhost:5432/mydatabase";
        String username = "myuser";
        String password = "mypassword";

        try (Connection conn = DriverManager.getConnection(url, "username", "password")) {
            System.out.println("Connected to the PostgreSQL server successfully.");
        } catch (SQLException e) {
            System.out.println(e.getMessage());
        }
    }
}
```

Here's the debugged code:

Chapter 9: Software Quality Management

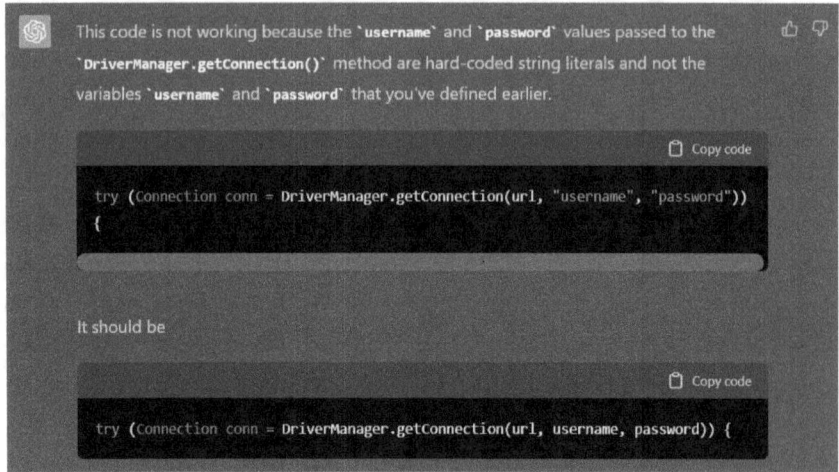

It even gave you the corrected code:

```java
public class Main {
    public static void main(String[] args) {
        String url = "jdbc:postgresql://localhost:5432/mydatabase";
        String username = "myuser";
        String password = "mypassword";

        try (Connection conn = DriverManager.getConnection(url, username, password)) {
            System.out.println("Connected to the PostgreSQL server successfully.");
        } catch (SQLException e) {
            System.out.println(e.getMessage());
        }
    }
}
```

Software Confidence Index (SCI)

At the end of a successful software release, the members of the project team get some breathing space to reflect on the completed project and ask some questions especially surrounding the success of the project or lesson learned from it; as we don't like the word "mistake" to label our shortcomings so we sugar coat this as "lesson learned". These questions are important to understand the level of success of any project but the irony is that most of the time, the way these questions are answered is very vague and almost impossible to quantify the success of that project. And as the saying goes – if you can't measure it, you can't improve it.

Imagine a large conference room, full of hardcore technical people, the managers, and potentially the sponsors or business users of the delivered software, for the project completion meeting (there are so many fancy names of this kind of meeting - lesson learned, retrospective, project closure, etc.). Everyone is eager to know how well or not so well the project was executed. The first question to start the conversation, usually is very simple which is most of the time asked by the Project Manager or Technical Manager which is "how have we done in this project?" Though the question is so simple the drama starts when people from different areas start to respond to this simple question. The responses fall on a wide range of the spectrum –

Technical Lead: "We've done a great job. The number of defects has gone down greatly ..."

Senior Developer: "It was good. The developers had written comparatively more code in this release (along with LOC, if available)"

Business Analysts: "The quality of business requirements was better; the developer didn't complain much about requirement issues in this release"

Business sponsors & User: "The software greatly simplifies our day-to-day work and improves the productivity of our employees" or "the performance of the software is not what we expected so it doesn't add many values in our business process".

Software Development Manager: "The throughput of the team has been increased significantly and we were able to deliver more software features compared to our previous release"

And this goes on and on.

There is nothing wrong with all the above answers and they all are right from the perspective of their business area. But the problem is how do you communicate success or failure to a different group of people, let's say the senior management in the company, do you think that they've enough time or interest to listen to all the answers of many lines written, the defect count, application performance or throughput of the development team? Moreover, how do you compare this result with your next or previous project or different software project in your company and the industry? So, even though the above kind of answers tell us the success or failure of the software, it is not easy to communicate to everyone across different interest groups. It is also not comparable across different software projects and certainly does not give a single measure point of success or failure that can be projected on a trend graph unambiguously.

Wouldn't it be simpler if we have a straightforward way of evaluating the success or failure or comparing it with other releases of projects which would be unambiguous to everyone and most importantly, measurable and quantified in a single number or index? My goal is to debunk the myth that software development is something that you can't compare one with another, even if the software is developed by the same team of programmers, because every software is a creative and unique piece of work that makes them incomparable. Let's see if all the dimensions (e.g., quality, productivity, reliability, performance, business value, end-user satisfaction, etc.) of the success of a software project can be combined into an index to measure them; let's call it Software Confidence Index (SCI). After all, we develop software systems that follow a predictive path of execution and can be measured in number so why not the success of the software that we've delivered should be quantified in number, to be exact, in percentage scale. So now let's change the answers that we had seen above in the conference room to a little different way and more unambiguous way:

"The project was great! The SCI was 85 in this release", or

"The release went somewhat well. The SCI was 75, we've room to improve in the field ...", or

"The SCI was 55. It didn't meet our expected goal. Let's talk about what went wrong ...", etc.

And if people have an interest in specific facts like defect density or software performance, that can be dug down in that meeting or a separate meeting with specific interest groups. The advantage of quantifying the success of the software through an index certainly is that it creates a new vocabulary to communicate across the board but on top of that, it can be used as a new goal-setting parameter for the entire team involved in the development and implementation of the software.

Now, the million-dollar question is - how this SCI can be computed. The SCI will cover both sides of the aisle of the software product, the technical side and business side. I would like to give equal weight to both the technical and the business factors, however, this can be changed depending on the project's importance on the technical or business priorities, as an example, for a software company, the technical factors may get higher weight whereas for non-software organizations may focus more on business values and end-users experience i.e., UX, rather than technical excellence. This should be determined by the organization's goals and priorities. There is no hard list of facts that should be considered to compute the index but it has to be consistent across the organization so that the comparison among the software SCI would make sense. Let's check out how it can be computed.

The index considers two kinds of factors: *Technical Factors and Business Factors i.e., End-User Experience*

The Technical Factors includes such as - code quality (duplicate code, unused variables, etc.), defect density, effective code coverage for unit tests, use of design documents and processes, use of standard coding practices (vulnerabilities in the code for security, memory leak, etc.), a benchmark of a load test result, etc.

- Each factor has threshold values to provide a point. E.g., If the defect density is less than 2 in 1,000 Lines of Code (LOC) then the point is 5 and if it is greater than 20 but less than 25 then the point is 1. The point between 1 and 5 is to cover the in-between values.
- Each factor has associated weights. The sum of the weights should be 10.

The Business factors i.e., the UX would be a questionnaire that is sent to the customers (the end-users) as a survey. The sample questions in that survey could be:

- Does the application have all the features delivered that were committed to the business?
- Does the application save valuable time and simplify end users' day to day job?
- Is it very easy and intuitive to use the features of the software?
- How satisfied are you with the performance of the software?
- How satisfied are you with the response of the IT Team to any problem experienced in the software?
- Overall, how satisfied are you with the software?
- How likely are you to recommend this IT Team to others with similar software needs?

Each question has points ranging from 1 to 5 where 5 is Extremely Satisfied or Agree and 1 is Extremely Dissatisfied or Completely Disagree. Similar to the Technical Factors, each business factor questions have weight and the sum of all weights is 10. For both the Technical Factors and Business Factors, the point would be 0 if the value falls outside of the accepted range.

Once all the factor values are known, then get the Software Confidence Index using the below equation:

$$SCI = \sum_{i=1}^{n}(T_i Point\ X\ T_i\ Weight) + \sum_{i=1}^{m}(B_i Point\ X\ B_i Weight)$$

Where T is Technical Factors and B is Business Factors

It is a starting point from where the discussion starts moving towards more of a rational and quantitative direction rather than vague and subjective discussion. This index is most effective and useful when the index is captured for a period that enables the comparison of historical data. This SCI can be used in many ways e.g., to create a benchmark in an organization, setting the goal to the software development team; compare the heterogeneous set of software delivered by an organization, etc. This isn't a silver bullet to improve the business confidence in the software but it definitely will set the course to improve the business confidence in the developed software.

There is also some skepticism on why SCI won't be any help to quantify software quality. The primary reasoning behind that skepticism is that the SCI does consider only a very few factors of software and its related development process and with that minimum number of factors the software confidence can't be computed into an index. Another quite appealing debate on its effectiveness is that software development is a creative work and it can't be measured or quantified. Let's look into each of the above allegations one by one.

Skepticism 1: Creative works can't be computed

I briefly touched on this in the prior section on Software Confidence Index but here I'm revisiting it as this seems to be a very appealing reason to most of the programmers. I don't disagree with the fact that programming is a creative work and it is very tough to measure the efficiency or compare the quality of software with another. Even the idea of quantifying the software or ranking software isn't new and managers sometimes use the concept of "pay for performance" and rank software engineers using the Effective Lines of Code (ELOC) which I wholeheartedly oppose as it creates an environment where writing more lines of code is seen as positive behavior however the opposite should be the truth. Moreover, the tendency to see oneself at the top may trigger bad practices of writing inefficient and redundant lines of code which could be avoided by using efficient coding practices such as, increased use of ternary operators over the "if-else" statement.

Even though I strongly oppose the use of ELOC but I always believe that consistently using few factors to rank developers and constantly monitor that process to get closer to the relatively perfect process would be effective to maintain the sanity in the competition (there is nothing called "absolutely perfect" but everything known as perfect in this world are more of "relatively perfect"). So if a good number of quantifiable factors are used consistently along with very few qualitative factors, a relatively perfect index can be achieved which will be no way perfect but would provide enough value to the software industry to start measuring software and can be compared against a benchmark index.

Skepticism 2: A limited number of factors can't be effective to compute the index

If this theory is true then a lot of famous numbers you see in the modern age would have disappeared. Take the example of GDP: The Gross Domestic Product is computed by using a formula where, in most cases, the production of a country is taken into consideration along with a few other factors. Do you think that government agencies can have the capability of counting every single product produced in a country? I know for sure that last year what I had produced in my backyard, at least 50 pounds tomato, almost same amount of cucumber, and a good number of other vegetables, weren't counted into the GDP and there are millions of people who do gardening every year and produces millions of pounds of vegetables in their backyard that go uncounted. There is some other way of computing GDP by not using production but through expenditure and other factors but for sure you'll find that no method can cover each and everything in this world. You will see the more striking number of factors in the computation of the inflation rate in a country. But the bottom line is if a method considers the same high impactful factors or group of factors over the period then the limitation of using a limited number of factors become less and less important in the process but the comparison of, in this case, the GDP and the Inflation over the period shows where the country is heading or if a country is doing better or worse within a macroeconomic environment.

PART IV
Technology *aspects of* Management

CHAPTER X

Chapter 10: Tech Skills of a Manager

Software Architecture & Design

As a Technical Lead or Technical Manager, you need to have a solid grasp of the various Systems Architecture and Design skills to participate, review or at the very least for the decision-making process. Here are the skills you should acquire:

- Understanding the Object-Oriented Principles (OOP). That starts with a solid understanding of Inheritance, Encapsulation, and Polymorphism.
- Augment your OOP knowledge with the SOLID (explained later in the chapter) principle and build an effective Object-Oriented Design (OOD) skill.
- Reusable Object-Oriented Design patterns such as Singleton, Factory Method/Abstract Factory, Proxy, Composition, Observer, Command, Chain of Responsibility, Strategy, State, Visitor patterns, etc.
- Application Design Pattern such as Model-View-Controller, Façade, etc.
- Software Architecture and Enterprise Architectures. Layered Architecture, N-tier (especially for Web Application), Client-Server, Microservices, Enterprise Service Bus (ESB), Service Oriented Architecture, Distributed Broker, Replication (Read/Write replica), Caching, etc.
- Database and Data Model Design: Normalization, Performance Tuning, Table partitioning, etc.
- NoSQL database design: Consistency-Availability-Partition Aware (CAP), Eventually Consistency.

Now, let's dive deep in some of the areas from the above list. Software Architecture is the area that covers the high-level interaction among the components of the software whereas the Design covers the mid-level interaction among the software sub-components that will ensure the code written by the developers conform to the predefined development and design standards. Let's cover some of the critical areas of software architecture and design and provide the resources for further learning.

Conway's Law of Software Architecture

Though this law has nothing to do with software techniques and technologies, this principle has a profound impact on what technologies would be used in software architecture. Conway's principle states: "Any organization that designs a system (defined broadly) will produce a design whose structure is a copy of the organization's communication structure." This indicates the strong bias that would influence the technical design based on whom you know and talk frequently. By being aware of this law, you would be more prepared when designing software systems. If you can liberate yourself from this communication constraint, you would be able to find a breakthrough solution to the problem that you would be given to solve. Read the original paper at:

http://www.melconway.com/Home/Conways_Law.html.

N-Tier Architecture and Layered Architecture

N-Tier (multi-tier) architecture distributes the responsibility of the software into self-contained components where each of them communicates through a defined service interface. Most web applications and client-server-based application software are designed in multi-tier fashion. In Layered architecture, specialization of multi-tier architecture, the software is designed in the way where the responsibilities of the software is organized in a layered fashion and enforcing that only the upper layer can invoke the services of the lower-level layers. The perfect example of Layered architecture is the Open Systems Interconnection (OSI) or Transmission Control Protocol/Internet Protocol (TCP/IP) model of computer networking. Learn more about Multi-tier architecture on *https://en.wikipedia.org/wiki/Multitier_architecture*.

Service-Oriented Architecture (SOA)

SOA is primarily to build a distributed software application that primarily runs over the web that works across languages and platforms. The fundamental of SOA is to create service components for a cohesive set of business functions and then orchestrate those services to automate the business functions. Learn more about SOA on

https://en.wikipedia.org/wiki/Service-oriented_architecture.

Microservices Architecture

Microservices is the latest software architecture that is gaining popularity across the business world. Microservices is an offshoot of Service Oriented Architecture that creates cohesive business service with no (or minimal) sharing with other components of the software. Similar to SOA, the Microservices interaction is also done through a defined Application Program Interface (API). The API Gateway is used to manage the orchestration, load balancing, transaction, etc. Microservices application uses the containerization for deployment. Docker is the de-facto standard for the deployment of Microservice.

Here are the simple steps to create a microservice in Java:

- Define the microservice's functionality: Identify the business logic that the microservice will implement and the APIs that it will expose.
- Choose a Java framework: Choose a Java framework that is suitable for microservice development. Spring Boot is a popular choice for building microservices in Java due to its lightweight and modular design.
- Implement the microservice logic: Write the code to implement the functionality of the microservice. This may include defining data models, database access, and business logic.
- Define the API endpoints: Define the API endpoints that the microservice will expose. This can be done using annotations in Spring Boot.
- Test the microservice: Write tests to ensure that the microservice is working correctly. You can use tools like JUnit and Mockito to write unit and integration tests.
- Package the microservice: Package the microservice into a deployable artifact, such as a JAR or WAR file.

- Deploy the microservice: Deploy the microservice to your chosen infrastructure. This may involve using a containerization platform like Docker or deploying to a cloud provider like AWS or Azure.
- Monitor and maintain the microservice: Set up monitoring and logging for the microservice to ensure that it is running correctly. You may also need to perform maintenance tasks like updating dependencies and patching security vulnerabilities over time.

To learn more about Microservices and Docker, go to

https://martinfowler.com/articles/microservices.html, *http://microservices.io*, and *https://www.docker.com/*.

SOLID principle

- *Single Responsibility Principle (SRP):* One class should do only one thing. No more, no less. In other words, a class should have only one responsibility. This principle aims to make the software more maintainable and easier to understand by ensuring that each class has a clear and specific purpose. The idea behind SRP is that a class should not have multiple responsibilities, as this can lead to tight coupling between classes, and make the code harder to change and test. By adhering to SRP, you can create more modular, flexible, and extensible code, which is easier to maintain and update over time. To follow SRP, you can start by identifying the responsibilities of your classes and making sure that each class has only one responsibility. If you find that a class has multiple responsibilities, you can consider refactoring it into smaller, more focused classes, each with a single responsibility. By following SRP, you can create code that is easier to understand, modify, and extend, making it a fundamental principle in creating robust, scalable, and maintainable software.
- *Open Close Principle (OCP):* The OCP states that software entities (classes, modules, functions, etc.) should be open for extension but closed for modification. In other words, you should be able to extend the behavior of a software entity without modifying its source code. The OCP encourages developers to write modular, reusable code that can

be easily extended without affecting the existing functionality. This can be achieved through the use of interfaces, abstract classes, and inheritance. By designing software in this way, developers can make their code more flexible, easier to maintain, and less error-prone. The OCP is important because it promotes the creation of code that can be easily adapted to changing requirements. By following the OCP, developers can write software that is more robust and can evolve over time without becoming too complex or difficult to maintain.

- *Liskov Substitution Principle (LSP):* Sub classes should be replaceable dynamically without impacting the application's stability. In other words, a subclass should be substitutable for its superclass in all contexts. To adhere to the LSP, subclasses must not alter the behavior of the parent class but may enhance it. This means that a subclass should accept the same inputs as the parent class, provide the same outputs, and follow the same basic contract. If the subclass needs to violate any of these rules, then it is not a true substitute for the parent class. The LSP promotes the creation of code that is more reusable and maintainable by allowing developers to substitute objects without fear of introducing errors or breaking the code. By adhering to the LSP, developers can write code that is more modular and extensible, making it easier to add new features or modify existing ones without introducing unintended side effects. Overall, the LSP is an important principle in object-oriented programming and should be followed by developers to ensure the creation of robust, maintainable code.

- *Interface segregation principle (ISP):* Interfaces should be segregated for cohesiveness to not to overload the implementers. In other words, consumer of a class should not be forced to depend on methods that they do not use. Instead of one large interface, multiple smaller interfaces should be preferred, each one targeted at a specific group of methods.

- *Dependency Inversion Principle (DIP):* Always work on Interfaces over concrete implementation. DIP aims to reduce the coupling between modules and promote loose coupling. It suggests that high-level modules should not depend on low-level modules and that both should depend on abstractions. Abstractions should not depend on details, but details should depend on abstractions. In simpler terms, DIP suggests that classes and modules should depend on abstractions, not on concrete implementations. This allows for greater flexibility and adaptability in the codebase, as changes to the implementation can be made without affecting the higher-level modules that depend on it.

Object-Oriented Design

Object-Oriented Design (OOD) is the low-level designing principles that are built on the object-oriented principles: Inheritance, Encapsulation, and Polymorphism. There are various modeling diagrams, such as, Class Diagrams, Sequence Diagrams, State Diagrams, etc. are widely used which are defined in Unified Modeling Language (UML). UML is covered later in this chapter in detail. To learn more about OOD, visit *https://en.wikipedia.org/wiki/Object-oriented_design*.

Here's a short note on the three foundational principles of OOD:

Inheritance

An object can inherit the properties (attributes and methods) of another object when defined in a parent-child relationship. This is the fundamental principle that makes Object-Oriented Programming so popular where the code reusability is achieved out of the box. This also opened up to the more dynamic behavior of the software system through runtime inheritance implication.

Encapsulation

The attributes and methods of an Object are made secure and provide stability to an object through encapsulation. There is the whole slew of implications of this principle however, this is the single most reason why an object-oriented design software is much more stable than a non-Object-Oriented software.

Polymorphism

Polymorphism provides the dynamic behavior to an object by allowing the object to behave differently based on the type of the instance. This also provides flexibility to the programmer by allowing various implementations of the Object's behavior based on how it is invoked. Method overriding and Method Overloading signifies the consequence of polymorphism.

Design Pattern

Design patterns are widely used patterns to solve design problems that are proven and used repeatedly in professional software development. Design patterns can be thought of as the recipe for a problem that can be taken as-is to solve the same problem with a different software development work. This is made famous by the publishing of the book "Design Patterns - Elements of Reusable Object-Oriented Software" by Gang of Four (GoF) that cataloged 24 object-oriented design patterns. This is the book that every aspiring software designer must read. In the meantime, please read the summary of the design patterns book (refer to the summary on *https://en.wikipedia.org/wiki/Design_Patterns*). Martin Fowler has written a book on enterprise application patterns that cover the application architecture patterns and is a useful read. Refer to Martin Fowler's website h*ttps://martinfowler.com/eaaCatalog/*.

Object-Oriented Design Patterns

I am listing here the most popular design patterns in terms of their usage and generic applicability for a majority of the application software: Singleton Pattern, Abstract Factory Pattern, Factory Method Pattern, Strategy Pattern, State Pattern, Composite Pattern, Decorator Pattern, Chain of Responsibility Pattern, Command Pattern, etc.

There can't be any better source to learn those design patterns but from the book: "Design Patterns: Elements of Reusable Object-Oriented Software", by Gang of Four (GoF).

Unified Modeling Language

Designing is the most significant part of the software development process that requires the ability to view the real-world problem in its abstract form. The designers analyze the problem domain and sketch a possible solution to the problem by breaking the domain up into different objects and their relationships. The designers design the system but the challenge is how they would communicate their thoughts to the programmers who eventually will write code to build the system. We need some sort of norms or protocols to represent the design of software which is unambiguous and has uniform meaning to everyone. Here the significance of standard notations comes into the picture. The most renowned and widely accepted solution to overcome this communication challenge is the Unified Modeling Language (UML), a non-proprietary, object-modeling, and specification language used in software engineering. UML includes a standardized graphical notation that may be used to create an abstract model of a system: the UML model. The UML has quickly become the de-facto standard for building object-oriented software.

System Design

Through System Design you define the architecture, modules, interfaces, and data for a system to satisfy specified requirements. System design can be seen as the application of systems theory to the design of software.

Even though it's not mentioned explicitly, system design is primarily involved in designing highly scalable, massive data driven and complex integration with other systems. As part of this process a detailed design of a software system is produced that specifies the hardware and software requirements, as well as the overall structure of the system. The system design process takes into account the functional and non-functional requirements of the system, as well as any relevant constraints.

The system design process can be summarized as:

- Define the problem: Identify the problem that the software system is intended to solve and define the requirements for the system. Once the problem scope is defined, conduct a feasibility study to determine whether the proposed system is feasible: technically and financially.
- Create design: Create a high-level overview of the system, including the major components and their interactions and a detailed design of the

system, including the specific algorithms and data structures that will be used.
- Proof of Concept or Prototyping: the design on paper should be validated using a prototype to prove out the systems.

Application Scalability

The paradigm of system design has changed in the last couple of decades where the most important aspect is the Scalability (Cyber security protection is at the same or even higher level of importance). The ability of a software system to handle an increasing workload with enormous amounts of data without experiencing a decrease in performance. Designing for scalability is important for ensuring that a system can continue to meet the demands of its users as the number of users and the volume of data increase over time. The ever-increasing volume of data (with or without labeling it as Big Data) and ubiquitous nature of the Internet with smart devices makes it imperative that the software that you design needs to be scalable both in terms of processing scalability and data scalability.

Processing Scalability

Few of the widely used techniques to design processing scalability are described below:

Distributed Architecture

By distributing the workload across multiple servers, it is possible to scale a system horizontally to handle an increasing number of requests. Breaking down a monolith application into a Microservices architecture is another most popular approach to implement distributed systems. Use of Kubernetes, Hadoop, AWS EC2 and Auto Scaling, etc. are readily available to implement distributed architected systems.

Load Balancing

Distribute the workload across the application and database nodes through Load balancing. There are various types of load balancing techniques that you can use: Application Load Balancing, Network Load Balancing, Database Load Balancing, etc. Most of the Cloud service providers come up with implementations of Load Balancing services that you can use readily, e.g., AWS Application Load Balancer, AWS Network Load Balancer, AWS Gateway Load Balancer, etc.

Caching

Caching can help reduce the load on the system by storing frequently accessed data in memory, allowing the system to quickly retrieve data without having to go back to the database or file systems stored on slower storage devices. Application and Database caching can be implemented through Redis, Memcached, Couchbase, etc.

Asynchronous Design

By using asynchronous processing, it is possible to handle requests concurrently, rather than sequentially, which can help improve the scalability of the system. Asynchronous architecture can be implemented using any Messaging systems like RabbitMQ, Kafka, Amazon SQS, etc.

Data scalability

Few of the widely used techniques to design database scalability are:

Database Sharding

Sharding involves partitioning a database into smaller pieces, called shards, which can be stored on different servers. This can help scale the system by allowing it to handle a larger number of requests. However, this also introduces major complexity to your system design. All major database providers support database sharding so don't think of creating your own sharding solution. MongoDB, Amazon Relational Database Service (RDS), Oracle, MySQL, Azure SQL Database, etc. supports database sharding.

Eventual consistency

If NoSQL is an option for the system being designed, use of eventual consistency helps to scale a humongous system to scale across the globe. A NoSQL database guarantees that the state of data would be consistent at a certain time threshold even at the expense of being available immediately. This is usually done using a concept called "quorum" where if a pre-set number of member nodes confirms an update, then the transaction is made permanent across the servers. The downside of that is that if a read-query is sent to the node where the update hasn't reached yet, the user will not see that latest data. NoSQL databases like MongoDB, Cassandra, etc. support eventual consistency.

Further reading for strengthening your skills in system design:

Books:

- Design Patterns - Elements of Reusable Object-Oriented Software by Gamma and others (Gang of Four)
- Patterns of Enterprise Application Architecture, by Martin Fowler
- Pattern-Oriented Software Architecture, A System of Patterns by Buschmann and others.
- Documenting Software Architecture by Clements, and others.

Web resources:

- *https://martinfowler.com/architecture/*
- *https://www.freecodecamp.org/news/solid-principles-explained-in-plain-english/*
- *https://reflectoring.io/*

Clean coding skills

As a manager you are less likely to write code but it's imperative that you must know what's a clean coding practice and what's not. If you're not familiar with this concept, I highly recommend that you read the book: *Clean Code* by *Robert C. Martin*. There can't be a better book than that on this topic. Until you read that, follow this basic rule for clean code.

> *"Always leave the code better than you found it"* - Robert C. Martin

Additionally, here are few clean coding best practices:

Do not Repeat Yourself (DRY): making sure to not to duplicate code- there can't be a worse crime in software development than duplicating code. Clean that first.

Naming convention: class, variables, functions etc. should be named meaningful. Always keep in mind that your code would be read by another human. So, write the code not only for machines but also for humans.

Class: should be small and strictly following the Single Responsibility Principle (SRP) i.e. "A class or module should have on, and only one, reason to change". Target achieving cohesiveness in your class i.e., "should have a small number of instance variables. In general, the more variables a method manipulates, the more cohesive that method is to its class."

Method or function: methods should be small and do just one thing. Also, make sure that the method doesn't create undeclared side effects.

Comments: write comments but do not think that your comment would fill the gap of a badly written code. If you have a clean code then the comment would automatically be reduced mostly to the purpose of the method or class.

Error handling: always use exceptions rather than return codes and never return null or pass null unless absolutely needed.

Unit Test: test your code through Unit Test code. Keep the Unit Test targeted and create a separate Test per assert. That also works as a check and balance force to keep your Class and Method clean.

Finally, the repeating advice is: read the Clean Code book if you haven't read it yet.

Refactoring

Refactoring can't be defined better than by the author of the book *Refactoring, Improving the Design of Existing Code*, Martin Fowler: "Refactoring is a disciplined technique for restructuring an existing body of code, altering its internal structure without changing its external behavior." You take an existing code base, look into it for improvement in certain areas and take methodical steps to overhaul it. If you better understand a concept through analogy then this is for you: Refactoring is like taking an old building structure and improve its habitability by using new building code, new design principles, new tools, new building materials, etc.[13]

Why to refactor?

The software code will inevitably get rotten after a span of a few years. This could be due to many reasons, some of them could be: the original developer's incompetence, shortcuts taken to release software "on time", changes in the technology, changes in the usage pattern, etc. Now as a new custodian of the codebase, you're tasked to maintain and enhance it. You can continue to keep-the-lights-on of the codebase without doing any refactoring to it; however, your codebase will rot faster if you just keep building on it. You have to revitalize the codebase to maintain efficiency. Nonetheless, if you're sure that this codebase has reached its End of Life (EOL) then you would not certainly need to invest into it. Be mindful though, it's not unusual to keep maintaining a software decade after its predicted EOL. Apart from that obvious EOL scenario, you shouldn't have any reason to stop doing refactoring. The benefits of refactoring include: Extends the EOL of a product; decrease the enhancement cost as it will be faster and easier to add code to it, test it, and deploy it; improved customer satisfaction with incremental improvements like better performance, less downtime for maintenance, faster production support, etc. Remember that easy-to-read code is always easy to debug.

When to refactor?

There's no beginning or end time for refactoring. Martin Fowler suggests that it's a developer's day to day job. However, to be practical, I would say that your first software release should not only have a Release note but also should have a "Technical Debt to Pay" note as well. Which is essentially like an "I owe you" note of a debtor, i.e., the developers. That "I owe you" note should trigger the refactoring and continue till you sign on the EOL epitaph of software code. If that sounds too structured and not smart enough then use this litmus test: if you are scared to touch a codebase in fear of breaking the code regardless wherever you touch it, then it should sound to you like an air raid siren and start digging the code to refactor.

I strongly recommend you to read the aforementioned Refactoring book if you really want to get the best out of refactoring. But to give you a glimpse I am providing a few bullet points so that you appreciate it and get excited to build your expertise, if you haven't acquired that yet[13]:

- Before you start any refactoring, make sure you have a solid test suite, be it Unit Test or Functional Test but have some kind of test code coverage. That will save you from frustration if not nightmare.
- Once you're ready with a solid test coverage, look for the "bad smells" mentioned in the Refactoring book like Duplicate Code, Large Class, Long Parameter List, Data Class, etc.
- Look into the methods if you are able to recompose methods through Extract Method, Inline Method, Replace Method with Method Object, Substitute Algorithm, etc.
- At Class level you can move features such as, method, field, etc. to a new Class.
- Other efforts in refactoring fall in the area of Organizing Data, Simplifying Conditional Expression, Making Method Calls Simpler, Dealing with Generalization, etc.
- Finally, don't shy away from refactoring at only code level, but also check if you need to refactor at architecture level if the usage, purpose and ecosystem have changed completely than the original intent of the software. If you can't afford to scrap the software and build a new one, embark in Architectural Refactoring and do it boldly.

Further reading:

Refactoring, Improving the Design of Existing Code by Martin Fowler

CHAPTER XI

Chapter 11: DevOps and Infrastructure

Chapter 11: DevOps and Infrastructure

As a Software Development Manager, you would most probably manage DevOps members or access to the DevOps team. Understanding the lingo and mechanism of DevOps is critical to manage your team's software development.

Configuration Management

This is also true just like all other areas of professional software development: what works very well in a small software program written by an individual, won't work when it is done on a larger scale. Here are some of the reasons why you would need to master the configuration management and build tools:

- First and foremost, in a professional software development project, the software would be developed in a team setting and written by several people. This creates so much dependency on each other that you won't be able to manage those dependencies without using a good version management tool.
- To make the software in a repeatable way as well as to manage the complex dependencies, it is necessary to use a build management scripting tool, such as Ant or Maven.

The most popular build management tools are Maven and Ant. Both are Apache projects. If you have a simpler project to manage where dependencies are less, you may use Ant build script. However, for more complex projects where dependencies are greater and need to share code and libraries across multiple projects, then Maven should be your choice of tool. You can go to the Ant and Maven sites to download and learn how to use them. The official sites of Maven and Ant are, respectively, *https://maven.apache.org/* and *http://ant.apache.org/*.

Continuous Integration

Continuous Integration (CI) covers primarily on building the code to make sure the working software is always in place and the codebase is conformant to the code quality and unit testing policy. There are many tools and techniques to implement the CI in a professional software project and some of them are covered here with the resource links. In a professional software development environment, usually, the software is built overnight and the build report is shared with the development team and management team through an email notification or a central web-based dashboard. Below are the list tools that you should learn architecture and mechanics if you don't know yet.

- Git (through GitHub or GitLab)
- Java Code Coverage (JaCoCo)
- SonarQube
- Jenkins
- Cruise Control
- Cloud CI/CD services e.g., AWS CI/CD

Cloud computing Infrastructure

The term "Cloud" is more of a marketing term than having any root in technology. In the early days, systems and network diagrams had been using a diagram of a cloud to denote the Internet and external networks. This term is now used to explain any systems or services made available through the Internet. Here's the more formal definition of cloud computing: Cloud computing is the way to take the IT infrastructure and applications outside of the company's Data Center. Additionally, sometimes it also has a connotation with the concept of utility computing where you pay as you use and billing is metered by your usage in terms of time, processing, storage, and throughput.

For a more formal definition, read the National Institute of Standards and Technology (NIST) publication:

https://www.nist.gov/news-events/news/2011/10/final-version-nist-cloud-computing-definition-published.

Types of Clouds

Based on where the cloud is deployed and who manages it, it is categorized as a Private, Public, and Hybrid cloud.

Private Cloud

Private cloud infrastructure is, as it says, private to a particular organization and only used to deploy the application of that organization. Though this sounds costly in terms of initial investment – which may top tens of millions of dollars – however, some organizations decide to opt for this option primarily due to the security it provides as well as to save the long-term cost of the public cloud. Mostly, financial organizations where security is the top priority build their cloud computing infrastructure.

Public Cloud

Public clouds are built and managed by companies to host other software and hardware systems. Some of the public cloud companies are Amazon Web Services or AWS (*https://aws.amazon.com*), IBM Cloud *https://www.ibm.com/cloud/*, Microsoft's Azure *https://azure.microsoft.com*, Google Cloud *https://cloud.google.com/*, etc. The biggest benefit of the public cloud is that there's no upfront cost of building a computing infrastructure and there's no maintenance cost to it. You just build your server or application and you will be billed to pay as you use. Once you're done with the application, just shut down the server.

Hybrid Cloud

A Hybrid cloud is the combination of both the public and private clouds. In this cloud deployment model, the organization would have its private cloud with a limited infrastructure capacity and burst into a public cloud, albeit securely, to meet the demand spike. Most of the major public cloud providers support the hybrid cloud model but among them, Softlayer (*http://www.softlayer.com/*), bought by IBM, is one of the pioneers in that area. This gives the security, economy, and control to the mission-critical systems of an organization.

Topology

The cloud topologies are roughly divided into three categories:

Chapter 11: DevOps and Infrastructure

Software as a Service (SaaS)

Cloud computing started with this model where a service provider makes the application software available to their customers where it is available to all on the Internet. Salesforce.com is the success story of SaaS and Google's all the services (Gmail, Google Docs, etc.) are the examples of SaaS where billions of customers, as well as companies, are using those services over the Internet.

Platform as a Service (PaaS)

In the PaaS topology, the Cloud service provider makes the underlying hardware and software stack available to the software developers and companies to build and deploy their application software. Amazon's Elastic Compute Cloud or EC2 (*https://aws.amazon.com/ec2/*) is the grand example of a PaaS provider where you can build a server with a particular version of the Tomcat or JBoss and start deploying your application.

Infrastructure as a Service

In the IaaS model, the underlying infrastructure server is provided to the customers and leaves the rest to them to decide what they want to build or deploy. One would use IaaS when they would need a standard server with a bare Operating System to do custom system design and deployment. This provides the flexibility and freedom to choose whatever the customer wants to build on top of it. Amazon's EC2 provides the IaaS solution as well.

AWS - pioneer and market leader in public Cloud computing

AWS has pioneered cloud computing to the serious computing world. Others have followed the path paved by Amazon. Here are the key architecture and features of AWS. If you would like to question why cloud computing is different from computing in your company data center, here's an analogy of cooking in your kitchen vs. eating out at a restaurant. For cooking in the kitchen, you need to have all the appliances, cooking ware, utensils, dining table, etc. bought, paid, and installed upfront. On the contrary, for eating out, you don't pay the cost of building the kitchen, pay the chefs, and keep paying the operational costs of tables at a restaurant - you just go there once in a week or as you may need. You just pay the service cost for each service, i.e., food and serving, you consume. The cost of food may be higher compared to if you were cooking at home. However, cooking at home requires the commitment of capital and operational costs to maintain the kitchen (and the very crucial and often forgotten invisible cost is the depreciation costs of materials). If you eat out, you can try out different cuisines and different dishes with little cost. Though it's a crude analogy, eating out is like using a public cloud for your computing needs where you pay for the services you consume and can try out new technologies and tools often at a very low cost.

The Well-Architected framework of AWS explains why and how Cloud computing is so different from traditional on-premise computing. It explains how cloud computing needs to be assessed.

Architecture: in a traditional on-premise environment, software and hardware architecture usually is a reasonably static decision made early in the design (even in the Agile environment). For instance: you would have chosen between Linux or Windows servers to procure servers and licenses accordingly. For Cloud, your Architecture decision can be truly Agile. You can change in the middle of your software development to go from one technology to another with a very little switching cost.

Operational: capacity planning is the most confusing and irrational planning that's done early at the project initiation - pretending everyone has the crystal ball to see the future. Cloud computing has changed it from a crystal ball approach to a "data-driven" approach. Don't pretend that you know the capacity growth demand for the next 3 years, but just monitor the growth and adjust the capacity near real-time or in a matter of hours as the demand changes. This major game-changer made Cloud computing so unique that no on-prem data center can beat that. This has enabled you to change the deployment process so drastically and reduce the risk of big bang deployment to "blue-green" deployment where you would build the new deployment instances and switch over as you feel comfortable without incurring the heavy cost of maintaining redundant production-grade servers.

Chapter 11: DevOps and Infrastructure

Infrastructure eco-systems: AWS Cloud Trail, AWS CloudFront, AWS Cloud Watch, etc. provides plug and play support to any systems you build in AWS without writing a single line of code. There are more such technologies in AWS.

Cost model: AWS or any cloud provider may claim that cloud would provide you with a better cost model however I would say that you need to be realistic based on the demand and capacity needed for your workloads. Think about Lease vs. buy a car - though they are not the same it gives you some sense. Both have their value proposition and depending on your long-term need and switching cost of technologies and infrastructures you may find yourself in two opposite ends of the cost spectrum.

Dev Ops

Development Operations or DevOps concentrates the group of activities that are required to build, deploy, and monitor developed software in an automated fashion. The skills required in the DevOps team overlaps with the skills of a software developer and the systems administrator. In a large software development organization, there would be a dedicated DevOps team however in a smaller organization, the software developers may play this role. Here are the areas and tools that are keys in the DevOps.

Source Code Management: for software code management, there are versioning systems that would be deployed and maintained by the DevOps. Git is the most popular SCM tool for both public and in-house software development.

Continuous Integration automation: some tools make the build and deployment automated and continuous. DevOps team configures those systems (e.g., Jenkins) to continuously build and run the integration of the software code and report if the application fails to build. It also integrates with various static code analyzer tools (e.g., Sonar https://www.sonarqube.org/) to monitor the code quality, unit test coverage, code vulnerability, etc. CI may also deploy a developed application directly to the non-production environment whereas the production environment would have more controlled approval-based deployment.

Continuous monitoring: after the code is deployed the DevOps team continuously monitors the performance of the application and provides timely information to the development and support team. To achieve that the DevOps team may create their monitoring scripts to monitor the Server's memory utilization, CPU utilization, storage availability, etc. There are various commercial and open-source tools available e.g., InspectIT *http://www.inspectit.rocks/* for application monitoring and Nagios *https://www.nagios.org/* for IT Infrastructure monitoring.

CHAPTER XII

Chapter 12: Software Security

Chapter 12: Software Security

As a Software Development Manager, you are responsible for the security of the software that's being built and is in operation. That alone should tell you the paramount importance of this topic. However, if I need a little more, I would add that your hard-earned reputation and branding or even your entire career can be ruined if you aren't aware of software security even after you have built the finest software on earth. Quite often we encounter the situation where Software Security has been an afterthought item which is to be checked off by the group that is responsible for the safeguarding of software security. That approach had been effective to some extent while the software was sitting in an isolated silo, totally disconnected from the outside world and accessed only within the boundary of that organization. But the ubiquitous presence of the Internet demands an immediate change in that approach. Time has come to shift the paradigm from reactive software security to a more proactive software security where security would not be implanted into the software after it is built rather the security would be a built-in feature organically grown from the very beginning of the software inception.

So, how can software security be built into the core fabric of software? This requires not just a change in the process and perception but a complete cultural change where the software security isn't the headache of the security guy sitting isolated in a cubicle at the corner of office, but a collaborative responsibility of everyone who are involved in the software development life cycle (SDLC) i.e., Analysis, Design, Development, Testing and Implementation.

The Goal of Software Security

Let's first clarify the goals of Software Security i.e., what we would like to achieve through this journey of secured software development. The goals are to achieve Confidentiality, Integrity, and Availability (CIA) in that Software. Confidentiality makes sure that the software provides access to the assets (i.e., data, processing, capability etc.) only to the authorized users on a need-to-know basis. Integrity is the attribute where the software ensures that the assets are kept in a consistent manner in every interaction. Availability is the characteristics that ensure a guaranteed level of availability of the software that's agreed upon by the software provider and the users. This availability is to be considered not by just the availability in terms of being accessible but accessible with a certain level of usability, throughput, and completeness. Each phase of the software would have to make sure that the CIA goals are met or, at least, taken into consideration.

Phases of Secure Software Development

The entire process to effectively incorporate the security in software can be broken into four phases: Planning, Execution, Monitoring, and Controlling. These four phases would effectively encompass the secure software development cycle, as depicted by the below diagram.

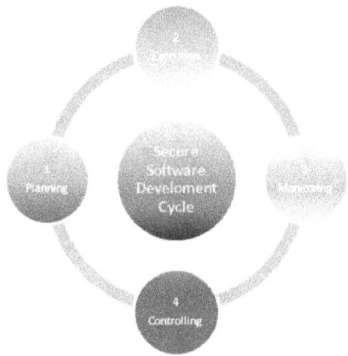

Figure-17: Phases of Secure Software Development Lifecycle

Planning

This is the most overlooked part when secure software development is taken into consideration. Most of the time, the goals of the secure software are not met due to the poor or, in some cases, lack of planning. The planning process starts with defining the goals of the software security and ends by creating a security execution plan. Here's a high-level depiction of the planning process and the desired artifacts to be produced through that process.

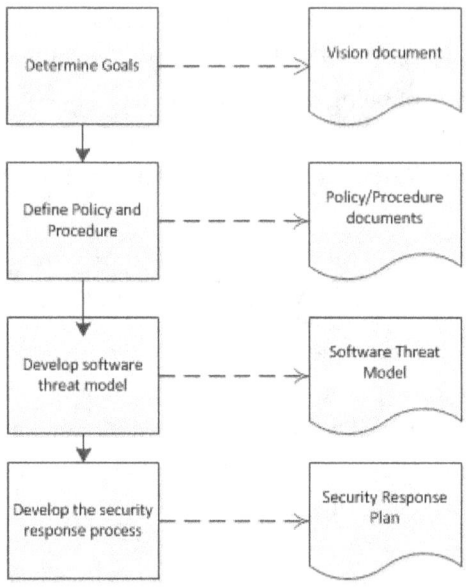

Figure-18: Planning process and the desired output artifacts.

Below is the deep dive into the detail of the planning process:

- The first step is to define the goals that the software security is targeting to achieve. The goals shouldn't be just a vague statement like "we want the software to be resilient and secured when under attack" but the goals should follow the SMART criteria i.e., Specific, Measurable, Achievable, Realistic and Time-bound. Here're few examples of SMART goals of Secure Software: "The software would have
  o zero code vulnerability as reported by the static code scanner,
  o Log 100% user's action at runtime.
  o Notify the security administrator within 30 minutes of a predetermined suspicious activity.
  o Shutdown all the services to access the "HIGH VALUED ASSETS" such as a database that holds customers personal information".
- Define a policy and procedure on how the software security activities would be integrated into the Software Development Life Cycle (SDLC).

One of the ways of achieving that is to define a "Tollgate" at every stage of SDLC and define the pass-through criterion. Here are a few examples of passing criteria:
- At the end of the Requirement phase, have a requirement review to verify that Security Requirements have been signed off by the Information Security Officer (ISO).
- At the end of the Development, an application code scanner is run and 100% critical vulnerabilities and 80% of Moderate vulnerabilities are resolved.
- QA has executed 100% Security Test Cases and is passed with provable evidence.

- Develop a Threat Model of the software being developed. A threat model is a way to understand and prioritize risks and evaluate mitigation possibilities. Steps to a threat model are: Identify assets, understand systems, understand threats, categorize threats and rank the threats".
- Few things need to be considered while analyzing the system (i.e., the software under construction) and the associated threats. Those are detailed understanding of the underlying technologies used in the software, vulnerabilities, and risks of the technologies being used, and the target market segment. Through the development of a threat model, the mitigation plan would be created. Usually, the high ranked threats are mitigated and moderate and low ranked threats are kept documented so that when the threats are materialized, an immediate response can be put in place.
- Making sure that the software development plan has incorporated the security artifacts in it.
- Develop and Security Test Plan & Strategy of the software in accordance with the Software Threat Model. The strategy would define how the software would be tested while being developed during the execution phase.
- Documenting the Security assumptions. Though this is true for every other aspect of the SDLC but for security this rank is very high and absolutely critical. The reason is, the software is usually built for a target

user group in a certain operating environment but eventually may end up being used in a completely different environment. As an example, software that was developed to serve internal customers within a corporate security peripheral may end up being used over the internet eventually when the company grows across geographical locations around the world. In that situation, the software's vulnerability should be re-evaluated but if the initial assumptions weren't documented, it may not be handled at the time of expanding the scope.
- The Security Response Plan (SRP) would have to be created as part of the planning process. The SRP would be used when the software would be in use. The SRP should elaborate the detailed procedure on responses when the software security threats are materialized as well as the roles and responsibilities of the security response team. Security Requirement has been signed off by the Information Security Officer (ISO) vulnerabilities and 80% of Moderate vulnerabilities are resolved.

Execution

In the execution phase, all the action plans created during the planning phase would be implemented. At every step of the standard Software Development Life Cycle (SDLC), the security aspect would be considered and implemented.

Requirement Analysis: the first step of the SDLC is the requirement analysis phase and security has to start from there as well. Along with the standard Function and Non-functional requirement analysis, a detailed security requirement analysis would be done. This security requirement analysis would start with standard authentication and authorization requirements of the software and then continue to develop the other requirements in light of the previously developed Software Threat Model. This is very important to document all the functional and non-functional security requirements (sometimes dubbed as abuse cases) so that the software can be verified to have those requirements built into the system. Below is the high-level breakdown of the execution process and the outcome artifacts:

Chapter 12: Software Security

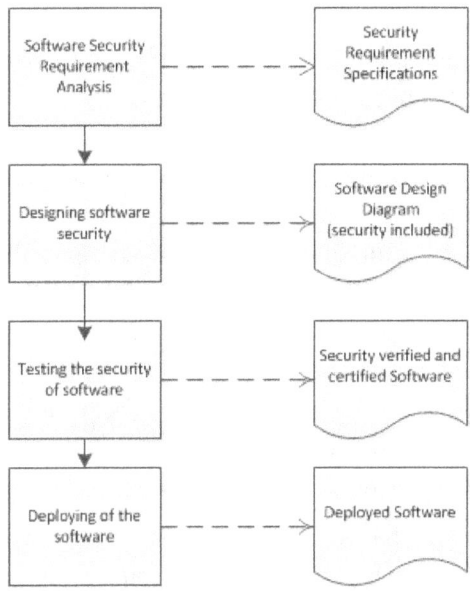

Figure-19: Execution process and the desired output artifacts.

Design and Development: the development of the software starts with the design of software. The security requirements of the software would be designed in parallel to the software's functional behavior. If the security requirements are not designed upfront in the process, the security would be used as a band-aid to the system rather than built into the system. In certain situations, the design of functional requirements of the software would be influenced by the security designs. As an example, the way the software would access the customer's personal confidential data (if available in that system) would be heavily dictated by the security requirement of the system. Here're few examples of design guideline to ensure the software security:

- Appropriate encryption has to be in place to prevent sniffing. This could mean the use of SSL, or if need further security, the second layer of

encryption can be enforced for certain assets that require a higher level of confidentiality.
- Data masking would be implemented to have the data visible to the people strictly as a need-to-know basis.
- Enforce the use of software libraries and frameworks that naturally prevents certain security threats, or if further security is needed, the second layer of encryption can be enforced for certain assets that require a higher level of confidentiality. As an example, the use of Object Relational Mapping (ORM) framework to access RDBMS databases will put an extra level of protection against SQL Injection.
- Every access and access-attempts would be logged.
- The movement of confidential data needs to be traced. The inbound and outbound data movements are to be logged with certain details (e.g., user ID, computer terminal, geographic location, time zone etc.).

During development, the developers need to use a software security static analyzer (e.g., IBM Security AppScan Source, or Veracode) while performing developer's unit testing. The software functionality can only be released when all the critical vulnerabilities are resolved. Though the zero-vulnerability reported by a static analyzer does not guarantee secured software, at the very least, this is a good starting point where all the known security issues are handled. Much of security vulnerabilities are exploited through a copybook attack of the well-known vulnerabilities. So, there's no excuse to slip the well-known vulnerabilities.

Testing: The incorporation of the security testing is necessary to ensure software security. The Testing process comprises two phases: Test Strategy and Test Execution. The Test Strategy has been developed as part of the planning phase and now during the Execution phase, the Security Test Cases are created and subsequently executed on the developed software. The successful execution of the Security test cases would be a precondition to release to software.

Deployment: This is the last phase of the SDLC when the other aspect of software security would be used to maintain the security of the system. It is imperative to say that the highly secured software can be deemed vulnerable and at risk due to the substandard deployment environment. The deployment security consists of:

- Physical security of the server and network systems
- Security of Operating systems of the server (through operating system hardening)
- Security of the platform consists of the application server, database server, web server etc.
- Security of the computer network
- Security of end users computing platform (when possible)

Monitoring

Unlike most of the other software development activities (e.g. analysis, design, development, testing etc.), the software security process does not stop at the completion of software development. Software needs to be kept under constant monitoring. The primary reason behind the need to keep the software under constant monitoring is that no amount of software security test can be enough to declare any software as free of security vulnerability or as free of security risk. To understand why it is almost impossible, take this hypothetical scenario: consider that the software uses the Advanced Encryption Standard (AES) 128-bit encryption method and at the time of the software delivery, the testing was done using the computational resources available and found unbreakable in a reasonable time period. But during the life of the software, the more powerful computer would be available at a much cheaper cost (Moore's law has guaranteed that) or a smart hacker would emerge who would break that encryption method using a smarter algorithm. That means the security group has to keep the software in monitoring to make sure that the software is not compromising the security on a daily basis. Below are some of the areas that would need active monitoring:

- The application code base should be periodically scanned for added vulnerabilities. This is very crucial, as even though the software may have been released with zero vulnerabilities but over the period of its

life, new code would be added and sometimes that newly added code could introduce new vulnerabilities into the piece of code that were previously deemed as secured.
- Monitoring the authorized users' access log if they are accessing the assets that they are authorized to. Sometimes the authorized users could gain access to the confidential functionality or data because of a software bug, administrative mistake, etc.
- Monitoring unauthorized access as well as the attempt to unauthorized access to the system. The logs of "attempt to unauthorized" access give clues to the security group on potential vulnerabilities where malicious users are trying to break in.
- The logs of the inbound and outbound data movement in the software should be under a constant monitor. The unusual movement of data may be an indication of the security breach.
- Server resource utilization has to be kept under constant monitoring. The use of CPU, memory, disk space, network I/O etc. could help to identify a potential abuse of the software. For example, if the software process is taking up unusually high CPU time or using more memory than the trend and doesn't have any reasonable cause for that, this gives a reason to investigate that high usage.
- Periodical Pen testing, Stress testing, and Load Testing should be conducted to probe the security vulnerability of the system.
- Prefer automated monitoring over a manual one. Manual monitoring is not sustainable. Manual monitoring can be put in place as an exception basis and only in the case where automated monitoring is impossible or not cost-effective.
- Software security should be quantified. Though it is very hard to tag a number to communicate the security level of software it is not impossible to achieve. The aspects of monitoring can be calibrated into a scale and compared against that scale. Through which it would be much easier to compare the improvement or decline of the software security risks. There is a downside of quantifying software security as it may give a false sense of security but the benefit of that outweighs the disadvantage.

- Finally, prefer the visual presentation of the monitoring results over text-based results. The human brain is naturally tuned to visual cues rather than text interpretation.

Controlling

There is no value in monitoring if an effective controlling process is not in place. In the controlling process, the outcome of monitoring would be used to take necessary action to prevent security threats and provide feedback to the planning process to improve the software's overall security.

The primary goal of this phase is to mitigate the potential threat or minimize the damage done due to the materialization of a potential security threat. For example, if monitoring of software detects an unusual activity of confidential data movement or a very high usage of server resources (CPU/memory), as an extreme measure, the software could be temporarily shut down to minimize the damage and then after proper investigation, this can be reopened if deemed secured. The control also involves applying software bug fix, security patch etc. in a timely manner to proactively thwart potential risks.

In conclusion, the software security in Software Development is more of a culture than a process and can't be attained at that level unless an organization fully appreciates the value of it. Software organizations should accept the fact that the cost is very high of not putting the focus on the security which could even go up to bankruptcy. Embracing the software security in every aspect of the software development life cycle is the key to have the security built into it. If the security is a module that is plugged into the software rather than built into the fabric of the software, the attackers can isolate the security module and force the software to compromise to their attacks. Every piece of the code must have to be security aware and only through that, a robust software security can be achieved.

PART V

Art aspects of Management

CHAPTER XIII

Chapter 13: The Art of Software Development

Chapter 13: The Art of Software Development

Software development is a subject of much controversy when it comes to putting it into a category of a particular academic faculty. People argue whether it falls under Science or Engineering. Both sides come up with great reasoning and justification why it should fall into one over the other. There are plenty of literary arguments for and against each of those faculties that you can find in the public domain. I would not go into that debate. However, just to set the stage for my next proposition I will put a simple commentary on that argument: like any engineering, Software development is to engineer software which can be touched and felt, in a literal sense if it's on a touch screen device, through the computing platform and its associated user experience; similarly, like Science - it's the discipline where the engineering isn't very much predictable backed by hard and fast engineering processes thus the outcome of the software development vastly depends on where it's done and with whom it's done. It has quite a bit of Art in it, if not quite a lot. And that leads me to conjecturally place this field into the faculty of Art.

Here's my reasoning on why software development is as close to Art as it is close to Engineering and Science. Software development is one of the very few disciplines of Science and Engineering where human psychology and their creative disposition play a key role to engineer a software product. At the same time, it is predictable when the human aspect can be set as constant or unchanged...Thus, the Art in software development is as important, if not more in some cases, as Science and Engineering.

A disclaimer before I dive deep into the art of software development: I assume that you want to be a part of the journey of building a software product that would make a dent in the grandeur of the software industry and not some mundane programming work.

Project initiation

At the beginning of the project, the vision of the software should be clearly communicated to the entire team. Have the software architecture diagram posted on each development room's wall, development wiki, and on the kitchen wall. Having the big picture always up allows instigating discussion as well as avoiding gaps in common understanding.

Effort Estimation:

When you are asked to provide an estimation of a new software project, never fall into the trap of "provide me just a ballpark figure" syndrome. You should provide the ballpark figure but only after you did your basic due-diligences. The Law of Large Numbers[14] is the name of the game here. Break the one-liner software vision or project goal into as much granular smaller requirements as possible and do the estimation at that level. Roll up to get the top-level ballpark figure. You would find that your optimistic estimations are getting compensated by your pessimistic estimations and in the end, you would get very close to the desired estimated date. Always remember- the more granular you go, the less margin of error you would find yourself in.

Architecture & Design:

Don't shy away from building new capabilities (like reusable framework) as part of your software development project. This is a trap where many software requirements push for a quick gain and get compelled to reuse existing "general purpose" software available in the Enterprise. This approach has both pros and cons at the same time. You would be able to create the working software early in the project i.e. being Agile, which is absolutely the right thing to do. However, you would be stuck in the limitation of that enterprise asset which may stifle you in your future functional and non-functional scalability. Here's the best practice:

Ensure the software architecture can decouple that Enterprise application when needed, in a cost-effective manner.

While utilizing the enterprise solution to implement your software systems, have alternate strategies. If you have leverage on that enterprise application development, submit a change request to that product development team early enough so that they can be ready at the time of your need. But if you don't have that influence or leverage then plan to replace that and build your own on a small scale in parallel. Though this may sound like a redundant cost which sounds right surely this will allow you to take you to the next stage once you find yourself stuck with the limitation of that enterprise application.

Never fall into the trap of "this would be a short project life cycle" and thus just build whatever you have in your hand. In a lot of cases, you would find yourself in an otherwise situation and continue enhancing the product for the next few years of your career. You never know how or where that product could pivot to grow into a giant system, or at the very least the demand from the customer may change to use this product for quite some time.

User Experience

User Experience or in short UX, shouldn't be confused by the graphical user interface through which the software is used. UX is to be built from within. The software that doesn't have any user interface, for example, an IoT device or a robot, also should have the UX built into it. In simple terms, UX to user interface design is what Smartness is to dress and cosmetics on faces.

The user experience can only be built into software if and only if the software development team has empathy for the users who would use the system. Put yourself in the shoes of the user and you would be able to better understand the pain point of using badly designed software.

Even though you may not have intended for or designed for the use of your software if designed resiliently, it would be used for purposes that you may never have imagined for. If you ignore that inevitable then you may have designed insignificant software that has no or little value on the grandeur of software engineering. Most of the time, the users find creative ways to use the features of the software that the developer may not have intended for.

Requirement Gathering

Requirements have to be analyzed in light of problem statements. There shouldn't be any requirements that are taken as-is without having clear and concise problem statements that it is trying to solve. Often you would get camouflaged solutions in the name of requirements from your user. Work collaboratively with them to peel off the outer layers of it and determine the true problem that the user is trying to solve. It's the skill of the requirement analysts to ask the right question in the right setting to determine the true requirement. Design Thinking can be used very effectively in this situation.

Requirements should be traceable in its entire life cycle, beginning from the inception to the operationalization. It may sound trivial but always have a permanent identifier (i.e. requirement ID) associated with the requirement so that it can be tracked and communicated unambiguously. Add a prioritization ranking to it so that you know what your user wants now and then next. Use numeric ranking and begin with 1 as the highest priority. Even though your business partner or your technical product owner may want to rank all of the requirements as "1", never allow that to happen. If you see such things happen in your team, you are sure to handle irrational and emotional situations rather than a rational and practical real world. Solve it first before you go further down in building the software solution.

Come up with the solution along with your end-user. For new innovative products, the product owner who has the product vision, engaging them from the get-go, would create a sense of joint ownership of the product. You would see the benefit of joint ownership in the future at times of turmoil in the project (which is obvious to happen) and you would find them as an alliance rather than your sworn enemy. The cost of that would be the sharing of the success and pride of developing "cool" software with end-users as they would also claim that they have built it. It's always better to be proud of software that is live and active rather than software that never saw the light of the real world.

Architecture and Design

Explore available products and platforms, especially to learn new ways of building software. You may use the product or platform for your systems architecture but most importantly, this is a great way to learn architecture. Architecture in the book or on paper is much more abstract to learn or appreciate than seeing architecture-in-Action in working software. Cloud vendors AWS, Azure, Google, IBM, Oracle, etc. have various implementations of new architecture on the cloud which is a great way to learn new architectural rigors.

Development and testing

Development should start very early in the game, never stay on paper or whiteboard level for more than a few weeks. While design diagrams would be on the design documents and presentation deck to communicate the solution, your utmost priority should be to constantly prove the new ideas in the software code - not on diagram and paper alone. This has two-fold values: test out any assumptions made during the design and people still give value to tangible things that they can touch and feel rather than need to imagine in their mind alone.

Test evidence is critical, be it developer's unit testing or SQA testing. It would avoid the "it worked before" syndrome which would deteriorate trust in the team.

Automation of unit testing is critical but you should have a hybrid approach along with manual testing. Use the 80-20 rule for the hybrid approach - 80% automation and 20% manual testing. The reason for the thumb rule of 80% automated test coverage is that it has costs associated with it to maintain automated test coverage so even it may sound cost-free or low cost but in reality, it is not (unless it's fully automated based on ML algorithms that learn from the data by itself). Also, having 100% automated test coverage may provide a false sense of complete coverage - remember that an automated test suite is not yet there to completely replace human intelligence. The automated testing would give you 80%

confidence that the software works but allow human testing to augment the remaining 20% coverage. In case of an immovable deadline, you may take a conscious risk if you would like to release software with 80% coverage of automated test cases or not.

Software Quality Assurance

Iterative testing is the key. Agile Scrum methodology is designed for that as part of Sprint. For legacy methodology, bake that into the project plan. Nonetheless, enforce iterative testing. You would have a regression test phase at the end of the development but that shouldn't be the phase to identify new bugs. Rather it's designed to provide full confidence that the complete suite of software solutions works end-to-end and not impacted by recent changes.

The SQA team should be empowered in the SDLC process. The Development and SQA team sit at an equal level in terms of hierarchy (though in many organizations SQA team suffers from the overpowering of Developers) but to be successful in software quality assurance, if needed, put them in higher authority to decide for the release of the software. Most of you know who are in development roles, development leads tend to squeeze the testing cycle when the development milestones are missed and spill into QA time. The reason the development leads and managers can squeeze the QA time is that often the Go Live date is set in stone and the only time you see is at the tail end of the SDLC and try to squeeze that (refer to Test Strategies).

Writing automation test scripts is efficient and cost-effective for software that is stable and not going through an active development phase otherwise the catch-up game to automation would eat up the fruit of the benefit of automation. Here comes the role of Artificial Intelligence and Machine Learning. Explore the possibility and feasibility (both in terms of viability and economy) of ML and AI in Testing. The technology isn't there yet but it's possible to create an algorithm that learns from the code and the defect history to augment the human tester to spend resources wisely. The only way to outpace the current pace of quality assurance is to move to a machine learning algorithm (supervised learning as primary and unsupervised learning as a secondary approach) that would truly automate the software testing.

Build and Deployment

If you use Agile methodology, this is a must-have, but regardless of your methodology, automating the build process should be your top priority. When you accumulate the total time to do build in a 6 months project, you would be astonished that it wouldn't be less than 20-30% of total project time that was spent to do build, if you do it manually. Often you see developers sitting in front of their machine doing the build for hours before testing the functionality can begin.

End to end deployment is preferred to be automated. Even if it's not, at the very least every build step should be automated. There are various tools for build and deployment automation (DevOps) - use any of them but use them.

Release Management

Release incrementally. If you use Agile software development methodology, this is the rule of the game "incremental working software". Even though you don't use that methodology, ensure the incremental deployment of functionality to production.

Operational Excellence

Early planning for end-user training and production Support is the key. Use that plan as part of your software development plan. Usually, the training part is no-brainer and gets done as planned. However, post-production support needs additional focus. This is so obvious that it may sound redundant to ask for but the majority of the software projects gets into crunch time at the end of the project (some of the reasons are: late identification of defects, scope creep, react to market change, etc.) and all focus turns into hitting the release date. Resources are sucked into the development, testing, and deployment. During that time, it's difficult for a software manager to execute the Operationalization plan. Here comes the courage of the leadership to stay focused on executing the operations plan. This is no brainer. Make sure the support process is documented, reviewed, and tested through simulation. Otherwise, the great success of delivering the software would be eaten up by the lack of managed support and through the chaos of post-production issue resolutions. Never for a moment assume that you won't have production issues in your software. Even though you have the best quality software product released, at the very least you would get a support call to explain how to use the systems for the first few months.

Debugging

Debugging is the true manifestation of the art of software development. Debugging can only be learned and can't be taught. Here are a few arts of software debugging:

- Look for what has changed before the software broke.
- Don't discount anything when you debug a software code. Most of the time, the software bug is caused due to a silly mistake.
- Use Deductive Reasoning to narrow down the issue until you isolate it completely. Though this is time-consuming this would guarantee the problem would be resolved.
- Use debugging tools to gather data and statistics. See the problem for yourself instead of consuming second-hand information by hearing from users or fellow developers. Most of the time, information that you would receive from the second-hand description, would curtail very important nuances.
- Finally, don't belittle the fact that intuition is the best tool humans are born with. Use it wisely and boldly.

CHAPTER XIV

Chapter 14: The Art of Software Development Management

Chapter 14: The Art of Software Development Management

This is useful if you are given tasks to lead or manage a software development team. Though management is a skill which is generally considered as a generic skill through which a manager gets the job done by a group of people, preferably a team, however, there are subtle differences in managing software development compared to other management work. I am covering the common best practices or you may call them as a rule of thumb, that will help you to apply those best practices without going through a costly trial-and-error process. You will also find those helpful especially if you are transitioning into a software development manager role from a non-software management role or even if you are completely new to management.

Technology Leadership

As you advance in your technology leadership role, keep these best practices in mind:

- New technology can simplify or enable what was previously considered difficult or impossible. Therefore, don't settle for the status quo, and always seek technological innovation to make things easier and more feasible.
- When deciding between prioritizing technology details or customer satisfaction, prioritize the latter.
- It's preferable to be agile when making decisions about using technology or tools, rather than waiting for the best option. However, be mindful of the pros and cons when implementing.
- Processes are implemented to aid technology management, so it's important to continually validate them. If a process impedes delivery, immediately re-evaluate it.

Team Building

This is the foundational area in Software Development Management that determines your ability to manage software development. Be very careful

Chapter 14: The Art of Software Development Management

at this stage and invest your best energy and utmost time to build your team.

Create a brand image of your organization and the product you would be developing. People, who would like to join you to do it just as a job, would never be the people that you would like to hire. The best people in software development always want to be on a journey to build history or make a dent in the timeline of history or at the very least do it because they love doing it. If you don't create a buzz or an attractive branding of your team, you would be hard-pressed to find the right people.

Use your network to spread the word that you are building a team. It's very important to tap all your networking connections to find the fit. The best people aren't always in the market - bring them out into the market to build your team.

The interview process is crucial. Never ask questions that only have a "yes or no" answer. You may ask the technical yes-no type of questions but if you want to understand their trait, better ask open-ended questions. Remember that you're not hiring for today's work but you're hiring for tomorrow's work and tomorrow's work never stays unchanged. Always ask open ended questions to allow them to express their inner creed. Questions like, "What is the greatest problem you have solved in your career?", "How do you solve a conflict in design decisions with architects and team members?", and "What are you learning nowadays?" Always back your verbal interview with the hands-on solution on the board or the computer to figure out if the person is only a talker or doer as well.

You may be developing with one technology today but you would be lucky if your technology stack or business model remains static for another six months. Even though you are lucky, your team needs to explore new functionality and new technologies to expand on the core product feature. So, do not "overfit" the candidate into your domain and solution stack. Generalize your organization's objective and try to find the best fit for that generalized model. Otherwise, you would find your "dream fit" candidate of no use when things change.

Chapter 14: The Art of Software Development Management

You can't change a person to be motivated if they are inherently unmotivated. You can motivate people to some extent with huge investment, however you won't be able to change them into a "star" unless they have the receptacle to be motivated. Your hiring process should tap those people who are self-motivated or have the receptacle to be motivated. Don't ask questions like "are you self-motivated?" Ask them to explain what keeps them motivated and you should be able to find if they are the folks that you are looking for.

One great software developer is at least 10 times better than a mediocre developer. You would need mediocre developers in the team to scale but the ratio should never fall below 80/20. If the ratio of great developers is below 50%, you should consider rebuilding the team or learn to remain happy with mediocre results.

Always keep hiring in the team - at the very least keep interviewing. Developers' churn is a norm so there should be a constant flow of new hires in the team.

Ensure the owner is assigned and known. This is the last thing you would like to see which is called: "it's not my responsibility" syndrome. The ownership and responsibilities are always better to put into black and white, however, if you are unsure for a certain period who to assign what and want to allow them to grow into it - that's also okay. Nonetheless, that period shouldn't exceed more than a few weeks, otherwise in absence of ownership there would be confusion, conflict, and finally chaos, none of which help to build a great software development team and great software product.

Human behavior is infectious: Motivated people are infectious in their way, just like the unmotivated people are infectious and create a toxic work environment. To create a motivated and healthy work environment, nurture and publicize the motivated people, and their actions while suppressing and isolating the unmotivated people and their actions.

Trust

Trust is something that you earn from others and not something you demand of others. If you are ever in a situation where you are asking someone to trust you, that is the symptom that you didn't earn that "thing" yet.

Demonstrate giving trust by giving others to own their decision making. If you can't trust your team to run autonomously without your day-to-day intervention, then the culture of trust would just be on paper not in practice.

Trust isn't free of short-term cost. You would have to stand your ground when you're hit by a few exploiters of trust. That will define your moment if you truly believe in trust-based leadership. There will always be one high-profile misappropriation which would push you to abandon trusting your team. Stay strong to reap the long-term benefit of a trust-based organization.

Respect

Respect that's tied into the hierarchical structure is not respect but obedience. Do respect your direct reports indifferent to power structure. Set a principle of "respect to all" in your organization of influence indifferent to the position and title and repeat it at every meeting and discussions.

Like many things in life, respect is reciprocal too so you would be rewarded sooner or later. However, if you work for an organization that doesn't believe in respecting human beings because and only because that they are human, not because of power structure, then it would be very difficult or may be impossible for you to reach absolutely to that state. Stick to your guns till your organization changes towards it.

Chapter 14: The Art of Software Development Management

Lead by example

Be on the ground with your team. Be it development of a complex feature, debugging of a production bug or estimation of a loosely-defined new project. Your team will not see you as an outsider but invested in them thus willingly following your leadership.

Emulate the behavior that you want to see in others. If you want the environment to be respectful, show it in your actions. As an example, if you want to see a collaborative team culture, for your next work accomplish that collaboratively with another member in your team.

Leading sometimes comes with a connotation of being "always right" which is not only true but is a fantasy created by Hollywood. You can't never be always right and not all of your decisions would turn out with a positive outcome. So, be honest and admit confidently when you were wrong and your decisions didn't turn out as anticipated. You will see developers in your organization start emulating that leadership style.

Decision Making through consultation

Even if you have the full authority to make a decision, bring the team into the decision-making process. This will help to build future leaders, get their heart in it and finally they will support you when you're hit by bad luck.

To avoid the bogged down situation, create a time-boxing approach of decision making i.e., the participants in the decision-making call would know that a decision would be made at the end of the meeting regardless. So, if some people want to slow down the decision-making process by "filibustering" the meeting.

Never leave the decision-making authority to others. Listen to all the options, evaluate the pros-and-cons of each option and facilitate the decision making or make the decision, if no consensus is feasible.

Once a decision is made publicly, never change the decision in private. If you have to change it for some absolute reason, go back to a public

237

meeting and remake the decisions. This will help you to earn a long-term trust.

Own the outcome of the decision, once it's made. When the outcome is positive and especially when the outcome is not so positive. Never blame others for the collective decisions made under your leadership.

Sharing information wisely

Leadership is sometimes defined by what you know or what level of access you have to the source of decisions or decision makers. As a software development manager, you will have access to organization sensitive information. So, you have to be pragmatic on how much information you share and when you share with your organization. There are no hard and fast rules for that but keep these in your mind while sharing information:

First step is to categorize information and share accordingly:

(a) Strategic information: Keep it at your level. Most of the time, this information would not only be unnecessary to the members who aren't involved in strategic leadership but would create confusion. E.g., market analysis report, company's future pivot direction, human resource rationalization strategy, etc.

(b) Tactical information: you review and make sure that sharing information wouldn't create unintended harm or side-effects.

(c) Other than Strategic or Tactical information: you may share this information freely to your team as and when needed.

Also, there are company specific information classification categories, such as: *Secret, Confidential, Company Internal, General,* etc. Those classifications are created and how to use those information classification is also defined. So, if you are handling those information classification, follow the company set rules and norms.

Use the *Need-to-know* principle for sharing information. If the information doesn't have any impact on the group, team or individual, then that

Chapter 14: The Art of Software Development Management

information shouldn't be shared. Sharing that would not only overwhelm the receivers but also may create unintended side effects.

Be careful of strategic information that has a bigger impact at organization level. That information should be either shared with everyone in the organization or keep it within the leadership until ready for sharing.

Equitable information sharing creates a trust-based organization in the company. Do not pick and choose people to share information based on who you have direct access with. Instead, use the need-to-know principle and make the publicly shareable information available through company internal memo, intranet website, internal blog, etc.

Don't be evil in withholding information for your personal gain. Even though this may sound philosophical in nature, you have to ask yourself to decide before you share. We, humans, are born with a natural constitution of state of purity and innocence i.e., Inner Good, so except a very few of us we would get the right answer. Act based on that. To make it little more objective, check if any of the below is true hence rectify yourself:

- Are you using information as a perk or as a tool to manage your organization or team? If you do that, then you're also violating the Trust based management style.
- Are you withholding sharing information based on who you don't like or who wouldn't be beneficial for you?

At times, you may have to obscure strategic and confidential information. Never lie or misinform your team. If you absolutely can't share, avoid that. If avoiding isn't an option, then share part of the information or a digest version of it in a manner that's not misinformation but also not exposing the confidentiality of it.

Technical prowess

If you're doing technical development work in parallel of being a manager, then you're already keeping yourself up to date but if you're not, then do the following:

- Keep yourself up to date with new technologies in software development. Read articles, books, watch training videos, join conferences, etc. Bottom line is – "keep learning". You can't afford to fall behind the technology while you're managing people
- If possible, be part of the review of the technical architecture of the software you are managing.
- Offer code review or join debugging discussion. This will keep you relevant to what's going on in the team.
- Don't shy away from reading "apparently unrelated" technology to your ongoing project. At the end technologies aren't just only technology but also concepts & ideas. So being exposed to completely different things will bring a completely different perspective to the software solution. I would suggest this to anyone in the software development industry or any industry whatsoever, and this is more relevant for people who are managing technology but not "doing" hands-on technical works.

Communication

There are three types of personalities when it comes to communication: over communicator, no communicator and just-right communicator. I don't need to tell you further what types of communicators you should be, right? in case I have to: just-right communicator.

When you're at the initiation of a project, building a new development team or similar situations, the more you communicate the better it is for the team. Once the project or team is settled and moving towards the set goal, minimize the communication otherwise that will promote confusion and chaos.

There's no either-or for written and verbal communication. Always use them as companions to each other. Especially, if you have verbal communication in a meeting, unless there's any real reason why not to, follow it through a written summary or follow up.

There's no substitute for face-to-face communication. Humans have historically evolved into "seeing is believing" mode so as a manager, you create the most impact through face-to-face interactions. Be sure to show your smiley face - it takes out the stress not only from you but also from the person you are talking to.

Pay full attention to the person you're talking to - face towards the person you're talking to and stay away from checking your phone, laptop, etc. You will get full attention in return.

Relationship

If you ask for the single most equity that you build through your management career, like the way you build equity in a home, I would argue that you build that equity of "Relationship". Without a strong relationship with other leaderships in the organization you wouldn't be able to create a significant impact in your organization.

Always look toward the long-term relationship over the outcome of each and every interaction and engagement through a transactional lens. If you want to win in every transactional event then you are risking losing the long-term relationship.

Relationships don't start when you need something from someone rather it starts from when you don't need anything from someone. This is a human behavior that they don't like to be "used" by others instead of being on an equal footing as a partner.

Don't confuse relationships with having a list of people who can help you when you need them. Rather, your relationship should be defined by the value you bring to the relationship through reciprocity. Those values could be your technical skills, being helpful, trustworthiness, shared values, common interests, social influence, personality, etc. creates the equity in your relationship that influences others to come to help when you need. So, build those equity in the relationship.

You shouldn't fuss when giving in to your counterpart's short-term demand. That's not losing but winning the hearts of others.

Metrics based management

This will alone differentiate you from a Hip shooter who reacts to every event intuitively and throws dirt in the dark to an effective manager who steadily improves from every event.

Define the metrics that are critical for your management. Neither everything can be quantified nor everything should be quantified. If you start to track how many times your developers take a break from their work and how many times they talk to each other, then that's nonsense. Rather quantify the outcome. Such as, how many times the build fails, how long it takes to build, how many times a bug is reopened, how much your team is delivering, what's the unit test and automated test case code coverage, etc.

Use correlation between and among your metrics. For example, if the code coverage of Unit Testing doesn't reduce the number of bugs identified in the QA testing or QA test automation doesn't significantly decrease the regression test time, your team is missing the fundamental purpose of unit test or test automation.

Something you can't quantify in a number such as what's the morale of your team however, use some kind of survey or pulse-check technique to quantify those valuable metrics to the extent possible. Use one-on-one meeting discussion and ask the questions and collect the data to add up to the team.

Automate, as much as possible, the capturing of metrics. If you're to spend 20% of your time just collecting metrics then it's not cost effective (nonetheless, you shouldn't stop collecting it, until you automate the creation of metrics) as you would not only be left with limited time to

Chapter 14: The Art of Software Development Management

manage your organization but you would not be able to continue that effectively for a long time.

Aggregate the metrics. This is key for your efficiency in management. If you have to always read the granular data points and come up with decisions every time, you would be inefficient and slow. Yes, you should have the granular data points to drill through however, you should use the aggregated data points. For example, if you are managing 4 teams and 20 Applications, you should've data points for individual team's and application's metrics which is then aggregated to the organization level.

Managing team through goals

Remember the divine hierarchy of Goals:

- Company Goals: Set by the company that you have limited control.
- Division/Department Goals: Set by the Division or Department. You may have some influence depending on your position.
- Team Goals: You define these goals by consulting with the team members.
- Individual Goals: Set by individuals and sometimes by you as a manager. However, the personal goals that you will never see fall under these goals.

Golden rule of goal setting:

Always define the goals along with hierarchy and in a staggered manner i.e., the higher-level goals should be expanded at the lower level thus a lower-level goal should never contradict with the higher-level goals.

Beware of Developer's Hour vs. Manager's hour

Developers need uninterrupted hours for development, especially when developing complex solutions. As mentioned in another place in the book, Programmers run an inbuilt compiler and execute the code like running in the debug mode in their head. When they code or do modifications in the code, they compile and run the code in their head to track output visually. Every time developers are interrupted in the middle of coding;

they have to do context-switching. Context-switching is like unloading the currently running code in the head and loading it in there which is very costly and wasteful. On the contrary, the work pattern of a manager fits just fine to the pattern of regular intervals at work. As a manager, keep that in consideration for meeting with developers: try to coalesce all the developers' meetings either early or late in the day so that they get long uninterrupted hours.

Multitasking: myth and truth

Multitasking is a feature that works well in computer processors and however, most multitasking works poorly in the human brain, unless that task is already hardwired for processing. This is called in psychological terms as: Inattentional or Autonomic processing. Here's a fact: Human brain is designed to process information from the environment every second, whether you want it or not. In fact, the human brain in one second processes 11 million bits that are environmental compared to just 11-60 bits that are intentional. The problem is that most of the work in Software Development isn't Autonomic rather creative. Moreover, when a task becomes Autonomic, then we automate that task. So, manage the multitasking as below:

- Determine your limit of multitasking and use that confidently. Whatever the number of tasks you can do in parallel, do it as that will make you most productive. If you're interested in increasing your level of multitasking and are able to do that, that's perfectly fine. However, don't set that your goal but set your productivity as your goal.
- Let your developers choose their level of multitasking. Don't force them to push them to work beyond their natural pattern of multitasking. Your goal should be to get the best productivity from them instead of reaching a certain number at multitasking.
- Sensory memory or register memory is opposite to permanent memory. If you need to create permanent memory, do not multitask. You may be fooled that you have acquired new knowledge while multitasking but

Chapter 14: The Art of Software Development Management

that knowledge would be stored in the short-term memory area and won't be transferred into the permanent area.

Collective (Team) knowledge

Just like an individual knowledge base is formed, when you have a team, there would be a Team's Collective knowledgebase. Recognize it and use it for the benefit of your organization.

Create a skill matrix, be it hard skills or soft skills, of your team. Know who is best at something and assign the work accordingly.

Do not concentrate knowledge and skills only on one individual. This would create unnecessary dependency and be the bottleneck of scaling the team. Also, too much dependency creates an imbalanced influence in the organization that will sway you from being equitable and fair to your direct reports.

Other Commonly Occurring Best Practices

Apart from the above categories, below are several more common best practices that you will find useful in your day-to-day management:

- Always keep the delivery schedule in front of your eyes (literally hanging the schedule on the wall in front of you) with minimal information such as the delivery date and/or possibly with the features to be delivered on the targeted date.
- Any issue or questions from the Development team and business users should be documented in some forms of a register. Without documentation, there is a high chance that you'll lose track of issues and queries and eventually would be dropped off of the final software deliveries. It is a "must-have" when you work with a geographically distributed team.
- Always assign a unique number (or ID) to every Requirements and Features. You can use any format ranging from a word document to a spreadsheet or just a text file but every requirement should be mapped to a number for traceability purposes.

Chapter 14: The Art of Software Development Management

- Make sure to track the changes (it comes as a feature if you use Microsoft Word) of the requirements and scope of work or at the very least track the changes from the base requirements by highlighting the delta. This will reduce the frustration from fishing for subtle changes within a large document. Moreover, it will reduce the chance of missing out the changes in the requirement as well as missing them in the actual implementation.
- You should never set priorities of a feature and, even if you have that in your mind, never say it first to users before the user expresses their need/want. Understand their needs first and ask the expected delivery date. Propose a delivery date based on business priority. You would have the chance to negotiate the date from there as needed.
- Keep versions of each and everything that the team produces: user manuals, software requirements, or design artifacts. For documents, keeping the version history is a must-have (with "track change" on). This should also have a summary of changes, who updated it, and when it was updated. For software and software packages, make sure to assign a version number. This will pay you off down the road.
- Never compromise with IT Security, such as access management. Enforce code review (and use of tools) to find such loopholes within the code. If you need to compromise for a short term due to a high priority business need, then get back to it as soon as possible. Otherwise, you will put yourself in unnecessary trouble. There is a real shortage of emphasis on security in software development. So, I have dedicated an entire chapter to cover how to develop software with built-in security (chapter: *Software Development and Security*).
- When you are talking about a deadline with the development team, ask them for the date, and negotiate it from there. Try to accept the estimation that the developers had asked for. Developers take the responsibility for their given deadline. But make sure when you review the status and if the team is lagging, this time, identify the root cause of the delay and set the date for the team accordingly.
- Measure the completion of tasks numerically. Never take the development status in terms of "nearly complete", "almost done",

Chapter 14: The Art of Software Development Management

"should be done in a couple of hours" etc. Just ask the percent of work remaining. If you use Agile Scrum, this would then be enforced by the Scrum ceremonies. In Scrum, you don't get the credit for a User Story if it is not 100% complete. Learn more about Agile in chapter: Software Development Methodology.

- Have a One-on-One session with all the members of your team. This is very helpful to get to know a lot of internal team chemistry that you would otherwise never get to know. You should cover the following three areas in that meeting - (a) what do you think about your performance and what you could do more; (b) What do you think the team should do to improve the team's performance and (c) Open discussion on anything related or unrelated to work.
- Measure the performance of the team and individuals quantitatively using consistent metrics. Have a 360-degree evaluation if feasible.
- Clarify the meaning of an apparently simple word that may have multiple meanings and may otherwise have a critical or adverse effect on your project deadline. For instance, when a developer tells you that she's going to "reuse" an existing piece of code, don't be shy to ask to explain the word "reuse". This seemingly obvious word caused one of my projects to be delayed by five (5) months where the developers meant "copy the code to the new module and modify it to make it work" whereas I assumed the literal meaning of that which was: "reuse the existing code from the existing module while refactoring the code to meet both modules' need". Sometimes the words - "it doesn't work" could have two meanings. One is "it doesn't give out the result as expected" and the other is "it is broken or it bombed".
- Programmers take pride in what they do so don't offend them with your knowledge or with your idea, especially if it is half-baked. Brainstorm with the team to come up with solutions and participate with the team – do not play the role of a boss. The creativity stops sprouting when the boss is in the conference room with an attitude of bossing around. Yes, you've to take the call to stop at a point where the discussion turns into an argument (which is very common in the software development world) but do it without offending one over another.

Chapter 14: The Art of Software Development Management

- Though this may sound subtle, never call programmers "resource". This offends the very nature of humanity (and programmers are human at work). I also have seen where managers call them "body". I have heard people saying that they need three more bodies, referring to programmers, for their project. It is very subtle and often the person whom you're referring to may not even notice that but eventually, it has a profound impact on your behavior on how you would treat a member of your team. Treat them as human. Nonetheless, I would strongly stand by the reality that the programmers are emotionally more invested compared to people in many other industries.
- Recognize the excellent performance of individual members in your team. There's a debate on where you should single out a person in a team to reward. I know that there are pros and cons of both as it may go against the spirit of teamwork. But I suggest recognizing the best performer of your team while having the team spirit as one of the selection criteria. It is like mixing Socialism with Capitalism where you create a sense of common ownership but also reward individuals for their extra mile run that goes beyond the set expectation.
- Remember Newton's First Law of Motion: An object at rest stays at rest and an object in motion stays in motion. The same is true for your team that you manage or lead. If the team is in a habit of failing the deadlines, they would keep it like that until you force it to turn around. So, make sure that every tiny little milestone, deliverables, or commitments are met. If you think that a deadline won't be met, reset it early enough (but don't wait for it to fail). Once your team is in the mode of meeting their commitments, you can relieve the pressure but keep the monitoring in place so that the hard-earned team's state doesn't get rusty.

Chapter 15: Ethical Software Development

Unfortunately, unlike other engineering disciplines, the software engineering profession is not subjected to the same scrutiny that mandates the coverage of professional engineering (PE) principles. This lack of standardized PE coverage has created a void that has led some software professionals to adopt questionable practices that remain unaddressed by academia and professional organizations. As a result, it is rare to find a course on professional engineering and ethics in computer science or software engineering degrees. Although attempts were made to establish "professional software engineers," due to the complexity of the field and its relative youth in the industry, it did not gain widespread acceptance.

Nonetheless, the scope of ethics covered in this chapter is much deeper in terms of the detail of the software development life cycle (SDLC) compared to regular PE ethics. The good news is that the majority of professional software engineers and programmers follow the common-sense ethics that exist in society and their respective states. However, there are few gray areas that are ambiguous enough to blur the line between ethical and unethical practices, knowingly or unknowingly. This chapter aims to cover those gray areas that are not addressed by the organization's policies and procedures for ethical business practices, such as insider trading, vendor gift limits and disclosure, and no bribery.

There are two types of remediation for these issues: individual and structural. At an individual level, every professional software engineer should take an oath, whether formally or informally, to refrain from engaging in such practices. Although individual commitment is crucial, there should also be systemic checks and balances to enforce it. Above all, transparency should be implemented, where it doesn't exist. Transparency is the most effective remedy for corruption. Keep requirements, solutions, architecture, design, code, and decision-making as transparent as possible (like a glass wall where everything can be seen through) to minimize the chances of such practices.

In each subsequent section, both individual and structural remedies will be provided as guidelines. It is best to offer an Ethics course as a prerequisite for obtaining a professional degree. Subsequently, a

Professional Engineering body should have the authority to periodically certify professional software engineers. Before delving into each area, let's first debunk the myth of job security.

Myth of Job security

The belief that having complete control over software development provides job security is a myth that many software engineers and managers fall into for a false sense of job security. Software professionals should pledge not to engage in this unethical and ineffective attempt. Job security has many variables and external factors, such as the economy, job market, demand for specific technologies, viability of an organization's business model, and more, most of which are beyond our control. Some people fight to protect their jobs, only to see the entire organization go bankrupt or a new technology make their field obsolete.

In the software development industry, job security comes from constantly learning and staying up-to-date with industry trends. Moreover, there is a significant downside to job security. If you are the only person who can develop and maintain software, your manager is likely to find the next person available to take the next cool project, while you are bogged down with your work. To be a little philosophical, we often sarcastically see our job as being more permanent than life itself. Moreover, if you think a little, being stuck in a single technology or role for too long may not be beneficial. Instead, you may miss out on opportunities that pass by while focusing on job security that may turn obsolete with the technology or job itself.

In summary, job security is not a matter of having full control over software development, but rather the constant pursuit of knowledge and skills in the ever-evolving industry. Professionals should avoid unethical practices and remember that job security is not guaranteed, as external factors often play a significant role in determining employment stability.

Requirement

You may even wonder how the Requirement can be in discussion for ethical software development. It starts with the requirement, just like the SDLC starts with the requirement. The product owner creates the scope or the requirement of the software in such a way that it either meets the need of the personal aspiration instead of putting the organization's requirement to the software development team. Types of practices are:

- Create requirements in such a way that it demands building software even though the similar capabilities exist in different software in the same organization. Through this the person gain control of the business processes, apparent job security,
- Create a complex requirement unnecessarily so that only that person understands it. Software requirements can have a complex solution but the need should be simple enough to explain.
- Finally, not documenting the requirement in its full scope and let it drip over the period of time. This is possible when the Product Owner has higher authority than the software development team and can get away with that behavior.

Individual Remedy: use Design Thinking to understand the right requirement (refer to the Design Thinking section). This way you would be able to unearth the true requirement that may be camouflaged by personal aspiration. Document the requirement even though it's not coming from the product owner and publish it to the product team. If the lack of a formal channel exists, send email; publish it on the team wiki, etc. Bottom line is having a timestamp on the requirement and associated communication.

Structural Remedy: There should be an independent review of the Software Requirement to confirm that there's no conflict of interest in the building of the vision of the software. This should be at the beginning of the SDLC and then continue periodically.

Chapter 15: Ethical Software Development

Architecture and design

The architecture and design of software is supposed to be really an objective thing that has no relation for or against any ethical software development. However, this is often the fertile ground of the most unethical that you would find in the entire profession of software development. This starts with the Architect or Software Development Manager's desire to enrich her resume and prepare for the next role or job in the career by filling the architecture with all sorts of nuggets that can be picked up later in the resume. The other immediate urge behind this practice is to show off colleagues and peers on how genius that architect or manager is. Shouldn't our architecture be open enough for future needs? The design should incorporate the functional (e.g., text/audio analysis, image recognition) and non-functional (e.g., scalability, performance) requirements that would certainly demand state-of-the technologies. Outside of that true necessity, these are some common types of unethical practices:

- "Any organization that designs a system (defined broadly) will produce a design whose structure is a copy of the organization's communication structure." - Melvin E. Conway, also known as Conway's Law. This is a nice way to say that our systems architecture follows our comfort zone. It's the reality of human behavior where we tend to mix with people with whom we feel comfortable. Though at face value, Conway's Principle sounds benign, it plays some role in it. The individual works with another team or other individual who has good rapport at the expense of architecting it right. We can't change that inherent behavioral pattern. I have seen software solutions or IT systems forced down the throat of a team because senior leadership has a vested interest or soft corner to that particular item. Sometimes, this seems to be the only solution available in the organization or in the market due to the lack of visibility (though that's incompetency) but the reality is not enough research was done to find the best alternative. To remediate it: expand the network of people you know thus expanding your horizon of systems available in the organization. Additionally, the

architectural review should be at organizational level with pros and cons of alternate systems for each solution.
- The professional journals and conferences often come up with the next big fad in the industry. The senior leaders come up with the mandate to the team that a certain new technology has to be included in the solution. If a simple workflow is required where it would never require end users to customize it or would change rarely, do not implement a third-party BPM service. Sometimes, to implement simple business logic, an intelligent Rules Engine is incorporated because that would be "cool" to present to higher authority.
- Many technologies exist to solve the same problem but to meet various non-functional requirements. The non-functional requirements such as, scalability, performance, testability, security, etc. are oversold to the end user. For example, Hadoop is absolutely an essential solution when structured and unstructured data needs to be processed at petabyte scale. But if the requirement is always structured with few terabytes and the performance requirement would not reach to the level where you would need a cluster of hundreds of nodes, then question the motive. Similarly, for a system that's highly transactional in nature with ACID boundary and a No-SQL database (probably to look cool) then question the motive.
- Nowadays, Machine Learning and Artificial Intelligence are two distinct fields that are heavily abused. People put all sorts of cool features of machine learning (e.g., Neural Nets, Natural Language Processing) in a system where there would be hardly any real use cases. Block chain has had its similar fad where it was tried to use as the silver bullet just like: everything is a nail when you only have a hammer.

Structural remedy: preventing this unethical practice through structural ways is rather very straight forward. Just like so many anti-corruption processes, have a check and balance with an independent body to avoid conflict of interest. Also, add Conway's Law as a checking point in the organizational design review process.

Coding

This is not the area where the bad practices arise the most. But it's always to write sensible code without adding more than necessary complexity and keep it readable. The best living documentation is a nicely written code with standard and meaningful naming convention. The cost of bad coding is not just bad practice but it's also very costly to maintain such code. Software maintenance is usually the bulk of the cost in the total lifespan of software and having badly written code is one of the root causes, after the badly designed software.

Individual remedy: Follow the standard coding guide, or create one if not available, standard code template, ought to be used religiously.

Structural remedy: Peer-review the code and use of code scan software (Veracode, Parasoft, etc.) can be used to remediate this.

Documentation

Documentation is not always the most fun thing for software engineers. Though most of the time the lack of documentation is caused by the nature of the work but at times, the lack of, or vague nature of documentation is also due to mythical job security. The poor state of documentation cuts the line of knowledge sharing which deprives others in the organization to learn about the software or the product.

Individual remedy: as mentioned in the "mythical job security" section, creating a good documentation of your software design and code won't necessarily create job insecurity but it would open up new job opportunities for you. People who are good at software development as well as documentation goes further compared to others in their career as they are in a better position to explain their work thus opening up new opportunities.

Structural remedy: If you use Agile Scrum, create the documentation (bare minimum) as part of User Story acceptance criteria and Definition of Done (DoD). For all other SDLC methodology, ensure the software documentation is part of the deliverable.

References

Transitioning into Professional Software Development. By Mohammad Masud, available at https://www.amazon.com/dp/B08BDSDYFL

[1] https://ns4business.com.br/tuckmans-stages-of-group-development/

[2] https://www.waldenu.edu/news-and-events/walden-news/2017/0530-whats-your-conflict-management-style

[3] http://www.orgcharting.com/wp-content/uploads/Matrix-Organizational-Chart.png

[4] https://www.pmi.org/about/learn-about-pmi/what-is-project-management

[5] https://rezaid.co.uk/sdlc-waterfall-model/

[6] https://en.wikipedia.org/wiki/Rational_Unified_Process

[7] https://en.wikipedia.org/wiki/Rational_Unified_Process#/media/File:Development-iterative.png

[8] https://www.researchgate.net/publication/220018149_The_Rational_Unified_Process--An_Introduction

[9] https://www.scaledagileframework.com/

[10] https://www.scaledagileframework.com/ https://www.atlassian.com/agile/agile-at-scale/what-is-safe

[11] https://blog.crisp.se/wp-content/uploads/2012/11/SpotifyScaling.pdf

[12] https://www.atlassian.com/agile/agile-at-scale/spotify

[13] https://reflectoring.io/

[14] https://en.wikipedia.org/wiki/Law_of_large_numbers

[15] https://www.scrumguides.org/scrum-guide.html

[16] https://www.scrum.org/resources/scrum-framework-poster

[17] https://www.visual-paradigm.com/scrum/scrum-burndown-chart/

[18] *Making The Team, A Guide for Managers, Leigh L. Thompson*

References

[19]*http://www.melconway.com/Home/Conways_Law.html.*

[20]*A Guide to the Project Management Book of Knowledge (PMBOK Guide), Fifth Edition, by PMI*

[21]*https://en.wikipedia.org/wiki/Program_evaluation_and_review_technique*

[22]*https://en.wikipedia.org/wiki/John_Kotter*

Index

360-degree feedback, 43
Advanced Encryption Standard (AES), 219
Agile, 103
Agile Software Development, 103
  Myth, 104
  silver bullet, 105
Ant, 204
Application Scalability, 197
Architecturally Significant Requirement (ASR), 125
Architecture, 208
Architecture & Design:, 225
Architecture and design, 253
Architecture and Design, 228
Asynchronous Design, 198
Availability, 212
AWS, 205, 206, 207
AWS Cloud Trail, 209
AWS Cloud Watch, 209
AWS CloudFront, 209
best practices, 164
Best Practices, 245
Build, 230
Burn down chart, 139
Caching, 198

Change Oriented Testing, 175
chatGPT, 179
CI/CD, 205
CIA, 212
Clean coding, 199
Cloud computing, 205
Coaching, 77
COCOMO, 157
code base, 219
Coding, 255
collocation, 120
Communicate Test Result, 171
Communication, 240
computer network, 219
Confidentiality, 212
Configuration Management, 204
Constructive Feedback, 68
consultation, 237
Continuous Integration, 204, 209
Conway's Law, 74
Creating Team
  Building team, 33
Creativity, 69
Critical Thinking, 51
  critical thinker, 52
Daily Scrum, 143

Index

Data masking, 218
Data scalability, 198
Database Sharding, 198
Debugging, 177, 231
Decision Making, 237
Definition of Done (DoD), 139
Definition of Ready (DoR), 138
Delphi Method, 161
Deployment, 230
Design Pattern, 195
Design Review, 126
Design Thinking, 117
Dev Lead, 23
Dev Ops, 209
Developer, 134
Developer's Hour, 243
Development, 228
Development Planning, 127
Disciplined Agile, 116
Distributed Architecture, 197
Documentation, 255
EC2, 207
Effective Communication, 60
    Communication, 60
    written communication, 61
Effective Decision Making, 52
    Hybrid decision making, 56
    Intuition driven decision making, 54
    Intution, 54
Effective Delegation, 64

Effective Listening, 66
effective meetings, 72
Efffective Decision Making
    Data driven decision making, 53
Effort Estimation:, 225
Elastic Compute Cloud, 207
Emotional Intelligence, 67
encryption, 217
Ethical Decision-Making, 64
Eventual consistency, 198
Execute Test, 171
Extreme Programming (XP), 112
Facilitation, 72
Firing
    Firing Management, 42
Fuel Innovation, 69
Function Point Analysis, 158
Functional organization, 81
Git, 205
goals, 243
Google Cloud, 206
GREAT meeting, 72
Heuristic Method, 162
High-Level Design (HLD), 125
Hiring
    Hiring management, 30
Hybrid Cloud, 206
Hybrid SDLC, 116
IaaS, 207

Index

IBM Security AppScan Source, 218

Influence Courageously, 70

information classification, 238

Information Security Officer (ISO), 216

Infrastructure as a Service, 207

Inner Good, 239

Integrity, 212

Iterative Development Process, 101

Java Code Coverage (JaCoCo), 205

Jenkins, 205

Job security, 251

Layered Architecture, 190

Lead by example, 237

Line of Code (LOC/SLOC), 157

Load Balancing, 197

Load Testing, 220

Manager's hour, 243

Managing conflicts, 63

managing software developers, 19

Matrix Organization, 81

Maven, 204

Mentoring, 76

Microservices Architecture, 191

Monitoring, 220

Motivating, 59

Multitasking, 244

myth, 244

Myth, 146, 251

Networking, 73

NIST, 205

N-Tier Architecture, 190

Object-Oriented Analysis, 149

Object-Oriented Design, 194
    Encapsulation, 194
    Inheritance, 194
    Polymorphism, 194

Object-Oriented Design Patterns, 195

One-on-One, 247

Operating systems, 219

Operational Excellence, 230

Pair Programming, 112

Pen testing, 220

Performance Management
    Individual performance, 40
    Team performance, 38

Phases of Secure Software Development, 213
    Controlling, 221
    Execution, 216
    Monitoring, 219
    Planning, 213

Physical security, 219

Platform as a Service (PaaS), 207

PMI, 85
    Process Groups, 86

politics, 73

Private Cloud, 206

Process Groups

Index

Executing, 86
Initiating, 86
Monitoring & Controlling, 86
Planning, 86
Project Closing, 86

Process improvement, 47

Processing Scalability, 197

Product Backlog (PB), 137

Product Backlog Grooming, 141

Product oriented management, 94
- Analysis, 94
- Construction, 94
- Design, 94
- Implementation, 95
- Testing, 94

Product Owner, 133

Project initiation, 224

Project Management, 84

Project organization, 81

Project oriented management, 88
- Project Closure, 93
- Project Execution, 91
- Project Initiation, 88
- Project Monitoring & Controlling, 91
- Project Planning, 89

Project Planning
- Project Change Management Plan, 90
- Project Communication Plan, 90
- Project Management Plan, 89

Project Risk Management Plan, 90
Project Timeline Plan, 90
Work Breakdown Structure (WBS), 90

Public Cloud, 206

Rational Unified Process, 102

Refactoring, 200

Relationship, 241

Relationships, 73

Release Management, 230

Requirement, 252

Requirement Analysis, 149

Requirement Gathering, 227

Requirement Management, 149

Respect, 236

Risk-Weighted Testing, 174

Roadmap of the journey, 21
- Developer, 21
- Development Lead, 22
- Development Manager, 24

RUP, 102

Scaled Agile Framework (SAFe), 113

SCM, 209

Scrum, 111, *131*

Scrum Demo, 144

Scrum Master (SM), 134

Scrum pre-requisites, 145

Scrum Retrospective, 145

Scrum Review, 144

SDLC, 215

Index

Second-Order thinking, 67
Security, 219
Security Response Plan (SRP), 216
server, 219
Service-Oriented Architecture (SOA), 190
Sharing information, 238
SMART, 77, 214
sniffing, 217
Software Architecture, 146, 189
Software as a Service (SaaS), 207
Software Confidence Index (SCI), 180
Software Cost Estimation, 152
Software Development Life Cycle (SDLC), 216
Software Project Management, 88
Software Quality Assurance, 229
Software Security, 212
Software. Confidentiality, 212
SOLID principle, 192
SonarQube, 205
Source Code, 209
Spectrum of Manager's role, 29
    Budgeting and Forecasting, 31
    Creating Team, 32
    Firing, 42
    Hiring, 29
    Performance Management, 36
    Reward and Recognition, 40
Spotify Model, 115
Sprint, 141
Sprint Backlog, 138
Sprint Planning, 142
Sprint Velocity, 140
SQA, 169
SQL Injection, 218
SSL, 217
stakeholders, 47, *58*
static analyzer, 218
Steve Jobs, 75
Strategic Leadership, 47
Stress testing, 220
System Design, 196
Team Building, 233
Team knowledge base, 245
Technical Debt, 201
Technical prowess, 240
Technology Leadership, 46, 233
Technology Roadmap, 46
Test Case, 170
Test Data Management, 170
Test Environment, 170
Test Plan, 170
Test Result, 171
Test Scenario, 170
Test Strategy, 170
testing, 228

Testing, 218

The cone of uncertainty, 154

Threat Model, 215

Triangulation, 150

Trust, 236

Unified Modelling Language, 195

Unit Testing, 127

Usage-Driven Testing, 176

Use Case, 150

Use Case Points Method (UUCPM), 159

User Experience, 226

User Story, 135, 150

User Story Points (USP), 160

User Story Task, 136

Veracode, 218

visual presentation, 221

vulnerabilities, 218

Water Cooler Moment, 78

Waterfall development methodology, 98

Well-Architected framework, 208

Working Remote, 78

written communication

Verbal communication, 60

END OF THE BOOK

NOTE

NOTE

NOTE

NOTE

www.ingramcontent.com/pod-product-compliance
Lightning Source LLC
Chambersburg PA
CBHW071352210526
45465CB00001B/63